Star of Wonder

For Su
WITH APPRECIATION AND THANKS

Star of Wonder

*Christmas Stories and Poems
for Children*

A Special Collection
compiled by Pat Alexander

Illustrated by Robin Lawrie

A LION BOOK

Selection, arrangement and introductory material
copyright © 1996 Pat Alexander
Illustrations copyright © 1996 Robin Lawrie
This edition copyright © 1996 Lion Publishing

Published by
Lion Publishing plc
Sandy Lane West, Oxford, England
ISBN 0 7459 2264 3
Lion Publishing
4050 Lee Vance View, Colorado Springs, CO 80918, USA
ISBN 0 7459 2264 3
Albatross Books Pty Ltd
PO Box 320, Sutherland, NSW 2232, Australia
ISBN 0 7324 1222 6

First edition 1996
10 9 8 7 6 5 4 3 2 1 0

A catalogue record for this book is available
from the British Library

Printed and bound in Spain

Contents

8 Donkey Tales   173

9 Loving and Giving   183

About This Book

Collecting and arranging this book of stories and poems has been great fun. I hope *you* will enjoy it too, whether you are reading it yourself, or being read to. I think you will find the stories as good to listen to as to read alone. This is a book for sharing – at home, at school, and in church too.

What is it that makes Christmas so *very* special? The excitement of presents? The food? The parties, when friends and families get together? Yes, all of these. Yet Christmas can be special without any of them. It's *why* we give presents and decorate our houses and cook extra nice food that really matters.

We do it to *celebrate* something – the very best thing that has ever happened to our world: that's what I, and Christians every-where, believe. Something that makes all the difference to the trouble and the hurting and the sadness that so often spoils things for us. Because at Christmas – the first Christmas, the real Christmas – Jesus Christ was born. The God who made our world came to be with us and help us:

He came down to earth from heaven
Who is God and Lord of all.

And although we can't now see him, he has never gone away.

A lot of people have helped me find stories, and I want to thank them all. There are so many stories about Christmas that I collected far more than would fit in this book. Some I was very sad to leave out. I am sure there are lots still to be found. So if *you* have a story or poem that makes Christmas special, and it's not in this book, do write and tell me. If you send your letters to Lion Publishing (the address is on page 4), they will pass them on. Who knows, together we may be able to make another book one day!

But till then, enjoy this one. Have a *very* happy Christmas. And, in the words of Tiny Tim, 'God bless us, every one!'

PAT ALEXANDER
Iffley, Oxford, 1996

1

'Once in Royal David's City'

The real Christmas – the first Christmas – took place long ago and far away.
Here is the story of the angel's message, the birth of Jesus, the shepherds and the Wise Men, as the Bible tells it. I have taken my extracts from the Revised English Bible.
The Bible text is followed by Bishop Timothy Dudley-Smith's beautiful retelling for younger readers.

A Time Like This

MADELEINE L'ENGLE

It was a time like this
war and tumult of war,
a horror in the air.
Hungry yawned the abyss –
and yet there came the star
and the child most wonderfully there.

It was a time like this
of fear and lust for power,
license and greed and blight –
and yet the Prince of bliss
came in the darkest hour
in quiet and silent light.

And in a time like this
how celebrate his birth
when all things fall apart?
Ah! wonderful it is
with no room on the earth
the stable is our heart.

The Bible's Story

From the Revised English Bible

The Angel's Message

from the Gospel of Luke, chapter 1

The angel Gabriel was sent by God to Nazareth, a town in Galilee, with a message for a girl betrothed to a man named Joseph, a descendant of David; the girl's name was Mary. The angel went in and said to her, 'Greetings, most favoured one! The Lord is with you.' But she was deeply troubled by what he said and wondered what this greeting could mean.

Then the angel said to her, 'Do not be afraid, Mary, for God has been gracious to you; you will conceive and give birth to a son, and you are to give him the name Jesus. He will be great, and will be called Son of the Most High. The Lord God will give him the throne of his ancestor David, and he will be king over Israel for ever; his reign shall never end.'

'How can this be?' said Mary. 'I am still a virgin.'

The angel answered, 'The Holy Spirit will come upon you, and the power of the Most High will overshadow you; for that reason the holy child to be born will be called Son of God. Moreover your kinswoman Elizabeth has herself conceived a son in her old age; and she who is reputed barren is now in her sixth month, for God's promises can never fail.' '

I am the Lord's servant,' said Mary; 'may it be as you have said.' Then the angel left her.

Soon afterwards Mary set out and hurried away to a town in the uplands of Judah. She went into Zechariah's house and greeted Elizabeth. And when Elizabeth heard Mary's greeting, the baby stirred in her womb. Then Elizabeth was filled with the Holy Spirit and exclaimed in a loud voice, 'God's blessing on you above all women, and his blessing is on the fruit of your womb. Who am I, that the mother of my Lord should visit me? I tell you, when your greeting sounded in my ears, the baby in my womb leapt for joy. Happy is she who has had faith that the Lord's promise to her would be fulfilled!'

And Mary said:

'My soul tells out the greatness of the Lord, my spirit has rejoiced in God my Saviour; for he has looked with favour on his servant, lowly as she is. From this day forward all generations will count me blessed, for the Mighty God has done great things for me. His name is holy, his mercy sure from generation to generation toward those who fear him. He has shown the might of his arm, he has routed the proud and all their schemes; he has brought down monarchs from their thrones, and raised on high the lowly. He has filled the hungry with good things, and sent the rich away empty. He has come to the help of Israel his servant, as he promised to our forefathers; he has not forgotten to show mercy to Abraham and his children's children for ever.'

Mary stayed with Elizabeth about three months and then returned home.

The Birth of Jesus
from the Gospel of Luke, chapter 2

In those days a decree was issued by the Emperor Augustus for a census to be taken throughout the Roman world. This was the first registration of its kind, it took place when Quirinius was governor of Syria. Everyone made his way to his own town to be registered. Joseph went up to Judaea from the town of Nazareth in Galilee, to register in the city of David called Bethlehem, because he was of the house of David by descent; and with him went Mary, his betrothed, who was expecting her child. While they were there the time came for her to have her baby, and she gave birth to a son, her firstborn. She wrapped him in swaddling clothes, and laid him in a manger, because there was no room for them at the inn.

Now in this same district there were shepherds out in the fields, keeping watch through the night over their flock. Suddenly an angel of the Lord appeared to them, and the glory of the Lord shone round them. They were terrified, but the angel said, 'Do not be afraid; I bring you good news, news of great joy for the whole nation. Today there has been born to you in the city of David a deliverer – the Messiah, the Lord. This will be the sign for you; you will find a baby wrapped in swaddling clothes and lying in a manger.' All at once there was with the angel a great company of the heavenly host, singing praise to God:

'Glory to God in highest heaven, and on earth peace to all in whom he delights.'

After the angels had left them and returned to heaven the shepherds said to one another, 'Come let us go straight to Bethlehem and see this thing that has happened, which the Lord has made known to us.' They hurried off and found Mary and Joseph, and the baby lying in a manger. When they saw the child they related what they had been told about him; and all who heard were astonished at what the shepherds said.

But Mary treasured up all these things and pondered over them. The shepherds returned glorifying and praising God for what they had heard and seen; it had all happened as they had been told.

The Visit of the Wise Men
from the Gospel of Matthew, chapter 2
Jesus was born at Bethlehem in Judaea during the reign of Herod. After his birth astrologers from the east arrived in Jerusalem, asking 'Where is the new-born king of the Jews? We observed the rising of his star, and we have come to pay him homage.' King Herod was greatly perturbed when he heard this, and so was the whole of Jerusalem. He called together the chief priests and scribes of the Jews, and asked them where the Messiah was to be born. '

At Bethlehem in Judaea,' they replied, 'for this is what the prophet wrote: "Bethlehem in the land of Judah, you are by no means least among the rulers of Judah; for out of you shall come a ruler to be the shepherd of my people Israel." '

Then Herod summoned the astrologers to meet him secretly, and ascertained from them the exact time when the star had appeared. He sent them to Bethlehem, and said, 'Go and make a careful search for the child, and when you have found him, bring me word, so that I may go myself and pay him homage.'

After hearing what the king had to say they set out; there before them was the star they had seen rising, and it went ahead of them until it stopped above the place where the child lay. They were overjoyed at the sight of it and, entering the house, they saw the child with Mary his mother and bowed low in homage to him; they opened their treasure chests and presented gifts to him: gold, frankincense, and myrrh. Then they returned to their own country by another route, for they had been warned in a dream not to go back to Herod.

After they had gone, an angel of the Lord appeared to Joseph in a dream, and said, 'Get up, take the child and his mother and escape with them to Egypt, and stay there until I tell you; for Herod is going to search for the child to kill him.' So Joseph got up, took mother and child by night, and sought refuge with them in Egypt, where he stayed till Herod's death.

Christmas Daybreak

CHRISTINA ROSSETTI

Before the paling of the stars,
Before the winter morn,
Before the earliest cockcrow,
Jesus Christ was born:
Born in a stable,
Cradled in a manger,
In the world His hands had made,
Born a stranger.

Priest and king lay fast asleep
In Jerusalem,
Young and old lay fast asleep
In crowded Bethlehem:
Saint and angel, ox and ass,
Kept a watch together,
Before the Christmas daybreak
In the winter weather.

Jesus on His Mother's breast
In the stable cold,
Spotless Lamb of God was He,
Shepherd of the fold.
Let us kneel with Mary Maid,
With Joseph bent and hoary,
With saint and angel, ox and ass,
To hail the King of Glory.

The First Christmas

TIMOTHY DUDLEY-SMITH

The Road to Bethlehem

Clip-clop, clip-clop, slowly the donkey plodded forwards. Joseph
walked beside him holding the bridle, trudging through the dusty
twilight. It had been a long day and a long journey – but there at
last were the roofs of Bethlehem.

Joseph's thoughts went back to that night, months ago now,
when first the angel of God had spoken to him in a dream and told
him that his wife Mary was to have a son. He was to be named
Jesus (which means Saviour) because, said the angel, 'he shall
save his people from their sins.'

Mary too had had a visitor. The angel Gabriel, one of God's
heavenly messengers, had come to stand beside her bed one night.

'Do not be afraid,' Gabriel had said. 'God loves you dearly. You
are going to be the mother of a son, and you will call him Jesus.
He will be great and will be known as the Son of God Most High.
He will be King over Israel for ever; his reign shall never end.'

The donkey stumbled on the stones. Joseph glanced up at Mary
and she smiled back – not far to go now. Really, thought Joseph,
she shouldn't be making this journey; the baby would come very
soon. But the government had ordered everyone to make the journey to the place of their birth to be counted and registered and to
pay their taxes. So here they were.

Bethlehem was noisy and full of people. They had nowhere to
sleep, and there was no room at the inn; every corner was full of
visitors. The best they could do was to find a stable with an empty
stall. At last Mary and Joseph, and no doubt the donkey, would
have a bite of supper.

And there was one thing more. By the light of the tiny
lantern Mary found an empty manger, the wood old and worn,
but solid and strong. She and Joseph filled it with the cleanest
of straw, and then there was nothing left to do. The noise of the
town died away. Only Mary and Joseph watched and waited,

holding hands in the darkness while the oxen munched and snorted in the stalls nearby.

God and his angels kept watch over the darkened stable. It was Christmas Eve.

Christmas Day

Out in the fields a wood fire was burning. It had been a big bright blaze at nightfall, but now it was only red embers and sparks dancing in the wind. Beyond the circle of firelight the hills were black under the stars; the sheep were just grey shapes in the darkness, and some of the shepherds were sleeping. A little way below them the townspeople of Bethlehem slept as well.

Suddenly an angel of the Lord appeared among the startled shepherds. Light burst upon them, blazing with the glory of God and the brightness of heaven. The shepherds gazed wide-eyed and open-mouthed, motionless with terror.

'Do not be afraid,' said the angel. 'I bring good news. Today in Bethlehem a Saviour has been born for you. He is Christ, the Lord. And this is your sign – you will find a baby lying in a manger.'

And all at once the night sky above them was full of singing angels, praising God and saying: 'Glory to God in highest heaven, and on earth peace for men on whom his favour rests.'

And then once more the shepherds were alone. Darkness and silence settled again on the hills. The fire crackled softly and a sheepbell tinkled. No one spoke or moved. Later the shepherds found themselves hurrying together down the path towards the town. 'A child in a manger,' they thought; and the place to look for a manger is a cowshed or a stable.

Perhaps it was Mary's lantern that brought them to the doorway in the hours before the dawn. All her life long Mary must have remembered those first visitors to her new baby – rough, bearded weather-beaten faces, patched cloaks and stout staffs, strong hands huge beside baby hands, and eyes still full of the angel's glory.

Soon dawn came to Bethlehem, and then full day. There were no cards and no presents, no decorations, no special food. But there was good news, singing and great joy, and the birth of Jesus.

It was a very happy Christmas!

*   *   *

Wise Men from the East

Clearly, they had come a long way. You could see that from their luggage, their jars, pouches and leather bags; and from their strange clothes and high-boned foreign faces.

These strange foreign visitors were Wise Men from the east. They had seen a new star in the night sky, far away in their own country, and according to their books and legends it was the sign of a king's birth – a very great king indeed. The star called them to leave their homes and make the journey to find the king; and they had precious gifts in their saddlebags.

Travel-worn and tired, they had come at last to the city of Jerusalem, where the cruel King Herod reigned. Now he knew nothing of the birth of any other king nearby. But his advisers told him of an ancient promise in the scroll of the prophet Micah that the king of Israel would be born in Bethlehem, just a few miles away.

Cunningly Herod sent the Wise Men to Bethlehem saying, 'When you have found your new king, come back and tell me, so that I may go myself and worship him.' But in his wicked heart he planned to kill the child and so be free of any rivals to his throne.

So the Wise Men set off on their camels. The star which they had seen in the east still went in front of them, until at last it shone directly over the house where Mary and Joseph were lodging with their son. The foreigners dismounted and fell on their knees to worship Jesus. They had found the king they had come so far to seek.

One by one they gave to Mary the gifts they had brought for Jesus: gold, precious and glinting in the lamplight; and spices, filling the room with the heavy fragrance of frankincense and myrrh.

They left as mysteriously as they came; but they did not go back to Herod as God warned them in a dream that Herod was not to be trusted.

But among the clothes and blankets Mary kept for Jesus, there remained the strange rich gifts by which she would always remember the strangers – yellow gold, sweet-smelling frankincense, and bitter myrrh.

2
Angels and Shepherds

Two stories in this section come from Bob Hartman's wonderful book *Angels, Angels, All Around*. He has such a way with angels! There are many, many stories that focus on the shepherds, that first Christmas night. There is space here for only a few.

The Surprise

BOB HARTMAN

The angel Gabriel sat in the corner and watched.

The girl was only thirteen. Fourteen, at most. Barely a woman, by the shape of her. With long, dark hair and bright olive skin. Not beautiful, but far from plain. Pretty.

The last thing he wanted to do was scare her. Like he'd scared that old priest Zechariah.

You did everything possible to ease the shock, Gabriel assured himself. No blinding flashes of light. No angelic choirs. You just appeared to him there beside the altar. He was in the temple, for heaven's sake! What better place to meet an angel?

But the old man had still been spooked. He clutched at his heart. He wobbled and shook like the smoke curling up from the altar.

'Don't be afraid,' Gabriel had said. 'The news I have for you is good. Your wife will have a baby. You will call him John. He will prepare God's people to meet the Messiah.'

The announcement was nothing like he'd practised it, of course. He'd had to blurt it out all in one breath because the old man looked like he was about to keel over.

Gabriel hugged his knees and scrunched himself back into the corner. He hated these surprise visits, and that's all there was to it.

The girl was whistling now. Doing her ordinary, everyday chores – as if this was some ordinary everyday, and not the most extraordinary day of her life.

The angel rested his chin on his knees. Think, Gabriel, think, he muttered to himself. She's young. But she's probably fragile like that old priest. So how do you do it? How do you tell her that God is about to change her whole life, without scaring her to death?

Mary began to sweep as she whistled. And as the dust motes danced in front of her broom, catching the sun and changing shape like dirty little clouds, Gabriel had an idea.

What about a vision? he asked himself. It always worked with the prophets. The dust rises and takes on the form of a man. 'Mary,' the dust-man says, 'you are going to be the mother of the Son of God!'

Gabriel shook his head, then buried it in his arms. No, no, no, he decided. Still too spooky. And besides, all it takes is a strong breeze and the poor girl has to dust her house all over again!

It was too late now, anyway. Mary had put her broom away and was across the room preparing dinner. Gabriel climbed up out of the corner and stretched. Then he followed her to the table.

Bread. She was making bread. And as she mixed the ingredients, another idea started to knead itself together and rise in Gabriel's head.

He could write the message in the flour on the table. Of course! An invisible hand, like the one that scratched those letters on the wall in Babylon. But it would have to be brief. It was a small table, after all. And there wasn't much time. Mary's parents were both gone, and there was no telling when they would be back. He wouldn't want to be surprised in the middle of his message. Gabriel hated surprises!

And then somebody knocked on the door. Gabriel jumped, startled by the sound. Mary quietly turned and walked to the door, wiping her hands as she went. It was a girl about Mary's age. Gabriel watched as they hugged and exchanged greetings. She had a brief message for Mary.

It wasn't long before Mary said goodbye and shut the door again.

I could do that, Gabriel thought. Knock at the door, like some unexpected visitor, and just give her the message... But what if she got scared and slammed the door in my face? Or what if someone passed by and saw us? She'll have enough explaining to do when the baby comes. She won't need to make excuses for some mysterious stranger.

And then Gabriel sighed. A long, frustrated angel sigh. Gabriel had run out of ideas. Gabriel was running out of time. So Gabriel sighed.

Perhaps it was the sigh. Perhaps it was something else that Mary heard. For whatever reason, she spun around and seemed to hang suspended in the air for a second – like one of those dust motes – her hair flung out behind her, her feet barely touching the

floor. And her eyes. Her eyes looked right into Gabriel's.

He hadn't noticed her eyes before. Brown, shining eyes. Young
and alive. They should have looked right through him, but they
didn't. They stopped where he stood, and they touched him.
Somehow she could see him. Somehow she knew he was there.

'Hello, Mary,' he said finally, because there was nothing else to
say. 'God is with you, and wants to do something very special for
you.'

Mary didn't say anything. But she didn't faint either. And that
was a great relief to the angel. She just stood there, shaking ever
so slightly, and stared at her guest. He could see those eyes swallow
up his words, see the questions and concern in those eyes as the
girl tried to puzzle out the meaning of his greeting.

'There's no need to be afraid,' Gabriel assured her, although it
was hard to know exactly what she was feeling. Was she trembling
with fear? Or was it more like excitement? Gabriel couldn't tell.
And he didn't like that one bit. This girl was nothing like what he
had expected. This girl was a bit of a surprise.

'Look,' he continued, 'God is very pleased with you. So pleased,
in fact, that he wants you to be the mother of a very special child –
Jesus, the Messiah. The Deliverer whom your people have been
waiting for all these years.'

Surely this would shock her, Gabriel thought. And he was ready
to catch her if she should fall. But all she did was sit herself down
to think. She played with the hem of her dress, folding and
unfolding it. She twisted her hair.

Say something, thought Gabriel. Say anything!

And finally she did.

'I don't understand,' she said. 'How can this happen? How can I become someone's mother when I'm not yet someone's wife?'

This was the last question the angel expected. This girl wasn't hysterical or alarmed. Her question was plain, straightforward and practical.

Gabriel cleared his throat and answered the question as best he could. 'The Holy Spirit will visit you. You will be wrapped in the power of the Almighty. And you will give birth to the Son of God.'

Mary had never heard of such a thing. And it showed. In her bright brown eyes it showed.

'Listen,' Gabriel explained, 'God can do anything. Think about your cousin Elizabeth. Well past child-bearing age. Barren, by all accounts. And yet she's expecting a son!'

Mary looked up at the angel and shook her head. She was still trying to take it in. But she wasn't afraid, he could tell that much. She was strong, this girl. A doer. A coper. A fighter. And when she finally weighed it all, Gabriel knew what her answer would be even before she gave it. Those eyes of hers were shining fierce and bold.

'I'll do it,' she said. 'I'll do it. I will be whatever God wants me to be.'

Gabriel nodded. Then he turned to leave. He reached out to open the curtain – the curtain between heaven and earth – and saw that his hand was trembling.

He turned back to look at Mary one last time. And in the mirror of her eyes, Gabriel saw a shocked angel face.

Mary smiled at him.

He smiled back. Perhaps surprises aren't so bad after all, he thought.

Then Gabriel pulled the curtain behind him and said goodbye to the girl. The girl who had surprised an angel. And who would one day surprise the world.

25

The Stars on Christmas Night

A tale told by the gypsies of Finland

Adapted from 'The Long Christmas'

RUTH SAWYER

There was a wonderful expectation in the world. All knew that a new and great thing was to happen, but none knew what it was. The stars in the sky looked questioningly at one another.

'What is it?' asked Capella on the right-hand side of the sky to Aldebaran on the left.

White rays flew to and fro; but Aldebaran answered quietly and secretly: 'Sister, I do not know.'

Vega in the northern sky asked Sirius in the lower sky: 'When will this wonderful thing come to pass?'

But Sirius did not know *when*, and Aldebaran did not know *what*.

The stars travelled around the Northern Star, and they thought every time they passed: 'This time, will this new thing come into the world?' But a thousand years went by and no new thing happened.

Then people began to move along the roads of Judaea. They were travelling to cities where they had been born, and many travelled to Bethlehem.

'Look!' shouted Capella across the sky to Aldebaran. 'There are many people passing and re-passing over the face of the earth. Can this great thing be about to happen?' And Aldebaran answered secretly and quietly: 'Sister, I do not know.'

Now there came to Bethlehem from Nazareth a carpenter, leading a donkey on which sat a woman. There was no room for them at the inn and they had to find shelter with the animals in a stable.

Up in the sky a great star was blazing, which had never been there before. A thousand, thousand stars were lost in wonder at it. Aegulus shouted to the king star, Orion: 'What does it mean?'

'It means that now is the time when the great and new thing will come into the world. But as yet, no one knows what it will be.'

Capella shouted across the sky to Aldebaran: 'Look! I see three kings coming from the east.'

And Aldebaran shouted back: 'Look! I see Herod trembling upon his throne.'

Vega shouted below to Sirius: 'Look! There are shepherds in the fields keeping watch over their sheep. They are wondrously afraid of the star. They know now what it means.'

And the Northern Star cried aloud: 'There is a new-born child in a Bethlehem manger; and hark, the angels are breaking into our midst with a great light and a singing of praises.'

Each star asked of his neighbour star: 'Is it the child that is born that we have been waiting for these thousand years? Has he come to fulfil the wonderful hope we all had?' And among themselves they whispered: 'Let us ask Orion.'

So they shouted across to the king of the stars, and to the earth below it sounded as though they were singing together; while Orion sang above the rest: 'Truly it is the new-born child who comes to fulfil our hopes!'

The Shepherds' Carol

ANON

We stood on the hills, Lady,
Our day's work done,
Watching the frosted meadows
That winter had won.

The evening was calm, Lady,
The air so still,
Silence more lovely than music
Folded the hill.

There was a star, Lady,
Shone in the night,
Larger than Venus it was
And bright, so bright.

Oh, a voice from the sky, Lady,
It seemed to us then
Telling of God being born
In the world of men.

And so we have come, Lady,
Our day's work done,
Our love, our hopes, ourselves
We give to your son.

'I Was There!'

DAVID KOSSOFF

My father and my grandfather were shepherds. It is a thing that runs in families. My sons own their own farms and their own sheep, but that is progress. I always looked after other people's sheep. Mind you, my sons are both clever, and quick in the mind, like my wife. She's always been rather a scholar. A good thing, for I can hardly read or write, but that was not unusual when I was younger. We were looked down on, I suppose, for often we had to work every day, ignoring the Sabbath, and with so many priests among the people, we were often told we were breaking the law. Though where the priests would have got their perfect lambs for sacrifice without us, I don't know...

People often tell me that mine was a dull life. Well, maybe. Looking after sheep *is* much the same each day. But many people have never seen the lambs play and leap, have never sat quiet on a hill and watched the sun. Or the moon. I like to watch the night sky, the moon and the stars. Once I saw, at night, a sight that very few have seen. Just once, but once was enough for any man. If a priest is rude to me, I always say to myself, 'It doesn't matter, I had that night and you didn't.'

I was about nineteen at the time, and, although it's now about fifty years ago, I remember it like yesterday. I lived with my parents, not far from Jerusalem, and I was one of a group of shepherds who looked after the sheep owned by the Temple. As I said, the sheep for the Temple services have to be perfect, and a great many are bred for food, too. We, our group, usually worked at night. On this night I'm talking about, we'd met up where we usually did, on the side of quite a big hill. We'd had a bite to eat and drink and were sitting talking. Around us, our hundreds of sheep. All normal and usual and quiet. Very restful and pleasant, those talks at night. It was a dark night.

Then there was a sort of stillness and a feeling of change, of difference. We all felt it. I had a friend called Simon, and he first noticed what the change was. It was the light. There was a sort of paleness. It was a dark night but suddenly it wasn't dark. We began to see each other's faces very clearly in a sort of silvery shimmering light. We seemed surrounded and enclosed in a great glow. It was the purest light I ever saw. The sheep were white as snow. Then, as our eyes began to ache with it, just farther up the hill from us the glow seemed to intensify and take shape, and we saw a man. Like us but not like us. Taller, stiller. Though we were still enough, God knows.

He looked at us and we looked at him. We waited for him to speak. It didn't seem right (we all felt it) for any of us to speak first. He took his time – as though to find the right words – and then he began to tell us what he called good news of great joy. Of a new-born baby, born in David's town. A baby sent by God, to save the world, to change things, to make things better. He told us where to go and find the baby and how to recognize him. And to tell other people the good news. His own pleasure in telling us filled us with joy, too. We shared his pleasure – if you follow me. Then he stopped speaking and became two. Then four, then eight, and in a second there seemed to be a million like him. Right up the hill and on up into the sky. A million. And they sang to us. 'Glory to God,' they sang, 'and on earth peace to all men.' It was wonderful. It came to an end and then they were gone. Every single one, and we felt lonely and lost.

Then Samuel, who was the eldest of us, said, 'Come, let us go and find the baby. David's town, the angel said; Bethlehem. In a manger. In swaddling clothes.' And off we went. We ran, we sang, we shouted, we were important, we'd been chosen. We were special. We were on a search, we had to find a baby.

And we did find him. We were led there. There was no 'searching'. We were led, and we saw for ourselves. Not much to see, perhaps. A young mother and her husband and her newly born baby. Born in a stable because all the inns were full. Poor people they were. The man was a carpenter.

Well, we did as we'd been told, we spread the word, and people did get excited. But not for long. Nothing lasts. We shepherds were heroes for a while, but then everyone knew the story. It was old news. Soon we were just shepherds again. Doing a dull job. But we were different from all the rest. We'd had that night. I don't talk about it much any more. But it keeps me warm. I was there.

Chester Carol

CHESTER MYSTERY PLAY

He who made the earth so fair
Slumbers in a stable bare,
Warmed by cattle standing there.

Oxen, lowing stand all round;
In the stall no other sound
Mars the peace by Mary found.

Joseph piles the soft, sweet hay,
Starlight drives the dark away,
Angels sing a heavenly lay.

Jesus sleeps in Mary's arm
Sheltered there from rude alarm,
None can do him ill or harm.

See His mother o'er him bend
Hers the joy to soothe and tend,
Hers the bliss that knows no end.

A Night the Stars Danced for Joy

BOB HARTMAN

The old shepherd, the shepherd's wife and the shepherd boy lay on their backs on top of the hill.

Their hands were folded behind their heads, and their feet stretched out in three directions like points on a compass. Their day's work was done. Their sheep had dropped off to sleep. And they had run out of things to say.

So they just lay there on top of that hill and stared lazily into the night sky.

It was a clear night. There were no clouds for shy stars to hide behind. And the bolder stars? For some reason, they seemed to be shining more proudly than even the old shepherd could remember.

Suddenly, what must have been the boldest star of all came rushing across the sky, dancing from one horizon to the other and showing off its sparkling serpent's tail.

'Shooting star,' said the boy dreamily. 'Make a wish.'

The old shepherd and his wife said nothing. They were too old for games and too tired, tonight, even to say so.

But they were not too old for wishing.

The old shepherd fixed his eyes on a cluster of stars that looked like a great bear. And he thought about the cluster of scars on his leg – jagged reminders of a battle he'd fought with a real bear long ago. A battle to save his sheep. He had been young and strong then. He'd won that battle.

There were other scars, too, mapped out like a hundred roads across his back. Souvenirs of his battles with that Great Bear, Rome. The land of Israel belonged to his people, not to the Roman invaders who were devouring it with their tyranny and taxes. So why should he bow politely to Roman soldiers and surrender his sheep for their banquets? Greedy tyrants. Uniformed thieves. That's what they were – the lot of them. And even their claw-sharp whips would not change his mind.

And so, even though he said nothing, the old shepherd made a wish. He wished for someone to save him. From violence. From greed. From bears.

The shepherd's wife had her eyes shut. This was the hardest time of the day for her. The time when there was nothing to do but try to fall asleep. The time when the wind always carried voices back to her. Her voice and her mother's. Angry, bitter voices. Voices hurling words that hurt. Words she wished she'd never spoken. Words she couldn't take back now, because her mother was dead. And there was no chance to say she was sorry.

And so, even though she said nothing, the shepherd's wife silently wished for peace, for an end to those bitter voices on the wind.

The shepherd boy grew tired of waiting.

'All right,' he said finally. '*I'll* make a wish then. I wish… I wish… I wish something interesting would happen for a change. Something exciting. I'm tired of just sitting on this hill night after night. I want something to laugh about. To sing and dance about.'

The old shepherd turned to look at his wife.

The shepherd's wife opened her eyes and shook her head.

But before either of them could lecture their son about being satisfied with what he had, something happened. Something that suggested the shepherd boy just might get his wish.

Like tiny white buds blossoming into gold flowers, the stars began to swell and spread, until their edges bled together and the sky was filled with a glowing blanket of light. And then that blanket of light began to shrink and gather itself into a brilliant, blinding ball that hung above the shepherds and left the rest of the sky black and empty.

Wide-eyed and slack-jawed, the shepherds dared not move. The wind had stopped. And the shepherds lay glued to the hillside, staring into that light. They watched it slowly change again. Shining rays stretched into arms. Legs kicked out like white beams. And a glowing face blinked bright and burning. The light sprouted wings. It took the shape of an angel. And it spoke.

'Don't be afraid,' the angel said. 'But sing and dance for joy! I have good news for you. Today, in Bethlehem, your Saviour was born – the Special One whom God promised to send you. Here's the proof: if you go to Bethlehem, you will find the baby wrapped in cloths and lying in a feed trough.'

The shepherds were still too shocked to speak. But that didn't keep them from thinking.

'Don't be afraid?' thought the old shepherd. 'He's got to be kidding.'

'A baby in a feed trough?' thought the shepherd's wife. 'Why even our own son got better treatment than that.'

'Sing and dance for joy?' thought the shepherd boy. 'Now that's more like it!'

And, as if in answer to the boy's thought, the angel threw his arms and legs wide, like the first step in some heavenly jig. But instead, he flung himself – could it be? – into a thousand different pieces of light, pieces that scattered themselves across the dark blue of the night and landed where the stars had been. Pieces that turned into angels themselves, singing a song that the shepherds had never heard before, to a tune that had been humming in their heads forever.

'Glory to God in the highest!' the angels sang. 'And peace on earth to all.'

Some plucked at lyres. Some blew trumpets. Some beat drums. Some banged cymbals. There were dancers, as well – spinning and whirling, larking and leaping across the face of the midnight moon.

Finally, when the music could get no louder, when the singers could sing no stronger, when the dancers could leap no higher, when the shepherds' mouths and eyes could open no further, everything came to a stop.

As quickly as the angels had come, they were gone. The sky was silent and filled once more with twinkling stars. The shepherds lay there for a moment, blinking and rubbing their eyes.

At last the old shepherd struggled to his feet. 'Well,' he said, 'looks like we'd better find this baby.'

The shepherd's wife pulled herself up, shook the grass off her robe and ran her fingers absently through her hair.

The shepherd boy leaped eagerly to his feet and shouted 'Hooray!'

When they got to Bethlehem, things were just as the angel had said. A husband and a young mother. And a baby in a feed trough.

A family much like the shepherd's, in fact. Was it possible, the old man wondered, for one so small, so poor, so ordinary, to be the Saviour? The Promised One?

Then he told the young mother about the angels. And that's when he knew. It was the look in her eyes. The look that said, 'How wonderful!' but also, 'I'm not surprised.'

There was something special going on here. The angels knew it. The mother knew it. And now the shepherd and his family knew it, too.

'Well,' said the boy as they made their way back to the hill, 'my wish came true. Too bad you didn't make a wish.'

The old shepherd said nothing. But he ran one finger gently along his scars. Was he imagining things, or were they smaller now?

The shepherd's wife said nothing. She was listening. There were no bitter voices on the wind now. There were songs – heaven songs – and the cry of a newborn child.

'Glory to God in the highest!' she shouted suddenly.

'And peace to everyone on earth!' the old shepherd shouted back.

Then the shepherd boy shouted, too – 'Hooray!' – and danced like an angel for joy.

A Greeting

AGATHA CHRISTIE MALLOWAN

In the Manger lies the Child;
Asses, Oxen, braying, lowing,
Cackling Hens and Cocks a'crowing.
Overfull the Inn tonight,
Up above a star shines bright,
Shepherds kneel beside their fold,
Wise Men bring their gifts of Gold,
Angels in the Sky above
Trumpet forth God's gift of Love.

Waken, children, one and all,
Wake to hear the trumpet call,
Leave your sleeping, 'tis the Day,
Christmas, glorious Christmas Day!

The Singing Shepherd

ANGELA ELWELL HUNT

*This story begins on Christmas night, but it doesn't stop there. For young
Jareb has a special part to play later on.*

Whenever he was afraid, Jareb sang. Singing made him feel better.

But his singing made everyone else feel worse. Jareb's singing
was dreadful.

Jareb was a shepherd. He helped his older brothers Ariel,
Samuel and Simon tend their father's sheep on the hillsides of
Bethlehem. Jareb loved the calm, quiet sheep.

But a shepherd's life can be frightening at times. Nights were
filled with dark shadows and eerie noises. The rumble of thunder,
the howls of jackals, and the hooting of owls caused Jareb to sing
a lot.

Ariel and Samuel hated Jareb's squeaky songs. 'But the sheep
like them,' Simon pointed out. 'They know no wild animal would
come near us while Jareb is yowling. Let him sing.'

So Jareb sang day and night. He even hummed in his sleep. His
brothers stuffed wool in their ears.

One cool night the shepherds settled their flock and lay down
to rest by the campfire. Ariel, Samuel and Simon fell asleep. Jareb
hummed off-key as his eyes grew heavy. The velvet darkness of
night wrapped around him, and Jareb yawned.

Before he could close his mouth, the sky flashed brighter than a
thousand campfires, and an angel stood right in front of Jareb. His
clothes glowed with a blinding blue flame. He shone like the sun.

Jareb was terrified. He tried to sing, but his mouth wouldn't
move. He heard his brothers gasp.

'Do not be afraid,' the visitor said. 'I bring you good news of
great joy for all people. This night a Saviour has been born in
Bethlehem. He is Christ the Lord.'

'Wh-wh-what?' Ariel asked. 'A Saviour?'

The shining man looked at Ariel and smiled. 'Here is a sign to help you find him. The baby will be wrapped in cloths and lying in a manger.'

Immediately the whole sky blazed with light, and hundreds of angels like the dazzling visitor filled the pasture and the hills. They were everywhere, in radiant white, and they seemed to look right at Jareb.

'Glory to God in the highest!' their voices rang through the still night, 'and on earth, peace to all people everywhere.'

The brilliant visitors shone brighter and brighter until they seemed to melt into a burning sky. Jareb and his brothers shielded their eyes. Then, in an instant, all was as dark as before.

'This is wonderful!' Ariel shouted, jumping to his feet. 'The Saviour has come. Let's go and find him!'

'How many babies in a manger can there be?' Samuel said, brushing grass from his clothes.

'The prophets said he'd come to Bethlehem,' Simon added, reaching for his sandals. 'Can you believe an angel came to *us?*'

Jareb didn't move. He began to sing softly.

'Come on, Jareb,' Samuel urged. 'Are you afraid? Too afraid to find this Saviour?'

'No,' Jareb answered. 'I'd rather stay here with the sheep, that's all.'

Ariel, Samuel and Simon turned and hurried to Bethlehem, their hearts full of excitement. Jareb stayed with the sheep, singing in the dark.

Jareb's brothers couldn't stop talking when they returned. 'You should have seen him,' Ariel told Jareb.

'You should not be such a coward, Jareb,' Simon added. '*You* were invited to see the Saviour, too. If God can send angels to invite you, can't he also give you a little courage?'

Jareb thought about the baby for many months. The more he thought, the more ashamed he felt. Why was he always afraid? Why did he spend all his time singing to silly sheep?

Jareb didn't want to be afraid any longer. One evening after the sheep were settled, he put on his cloak.

'Where are you going?' asked Samuel. 'It will be dark soon.'

'I am going to find that baby,' Jareb answered. And off he went to Bethlehem, singing off-key.

Jareb had no idea how to find a child who had been born so many months before. He didn't even know if the family still lived in Bethlehem. He prayed that God would guide his footsteps.

The road into Bethlehem was crowded. A rich caravan of men and camels was coming out of the town, and Jareb had to stop and wait for it to pass. Suddenly a young camel slipped away from the others and bolted straight at Jareb.

'Quick! Stop that camel!'

Without thinking, Jareb caught the rope dangling from the camel's neck.

'Thank you, young man,' the servant said, taking the camel from Jareb. 'My masters are rich men, but they would be angry if I lost their prized camel. Although,' the servant scratched his head, 'since we left the child's house, my masters have not stopped smiling.'

'Oh?' Jareb asked, hardly daring to hope. 'What child is that?'

'A wonderful, beautiful child.' The servant smiled at Jareb. 'He will be a great king some day, my masters say. We have come a great distance to find him.'

Jareb's heart beat faster as the servant told him where to find the child. Could this be the Saviour?

It was very dark when Jareb found the house the servant had described. No lamplight flickered from the window, and Jareb thought everyone was asleep. Suddenly the door opened. A bearded man looked quickly up and down the street.

Jareb took a deep breath and stepped forward.

'Please, sir,' he said, 'may I see the child?'

The bearded man frowned. 'Who sent you?' he asked.

Jareb felt his cheeks burning with shame. 'An angel. Many months ago. But I was afraid to come.'

The man pulled Jareb inside.

'I am Joseph,' he said. 'Here is my wife Mary. And this is Jesus.'

In the starlight streaming through the window, Jareb saw a young woman holding a sleeping child. The woman smiled shyly at Jareb.

Joseph spoke again. 'An angel has warned me that King Herod will send soldiers to kill all baby boys in Bethlehem. Mary and I must take Jesus away from here. But there may be soldiers at the city gate already. You must help us.'

'Soldiers?' Jareb felt his knees begin to quiver. 'Killing? King Herod?' Jareb's words trailed off, and he began to hum nervously.

'We must leave tonight,' Joseph interrupted. 'God has sent you to us. Will you help?'

Jareb thought for a moment. Then he pulled a rough shawl from his shoulder. 'This is a sling for newborn lambs,' he explained. 'With it I could carry Jesus outside the city. No one would expect me to be carrying a baby.'

Joseph smiled. 'Your plan is good, my young friend,' he said. Joseph and Mary carefully placed Jesus in the sling.

'There is a well outside the city gate,' Jareb whispered. 'I will meet you there.'

Mary and Joseph slipped out into the darkness. Jareb carefully shifted the sling onto his shoulder and peered down the street. He could hear noise far away – screaming and the clash of swords. Jareb was more frightened than he had ever been in his life. He prayed the baby wouldn't cry. Then he set out for the city gate, humming softly as he walked.

At the gate, a rough guard stepped in front of Jareb and squinted down at him. 'We are looking for babies,' he growled, 'baby boys. What's that you're carrying?'

'Please, sir,' Jareb stammered. 'I'm... I'm just a shepherd. And this is a sling for carrying lambs.'

Jareb felt his fingers begin to tremble. He squeezed the strap of the sling and tried to smile. 'I'm famous for my sheep songs. Just listen.'

Jareb burst into song. Fear made his voice louder and scratchier and even more out of tune than usual. The guard shuddered in disgust and covered his ears. 'Arrgh!' he shouted. 'Away with you, crazy shepherd. Stop that awful racket!'

Outside the city, Joseph and Mary were waiting anxiously by the well. Jareb gently lifted Jesus from the sling.

'Here's your little lamb,' he said, placing the child in Mary's arms. Jareb laughed. 'Look how he smiles at the world's worst singer!'

'You are a very brave young man.' Mary smiled and her eyes filled with tears. 'And your voice is a blessing from God.'

Jareb watched until the small family disappeared on the road, then he turned to the fields where his sheep waited.

Jareb's ears rang with Mary's words, 'You are a brave young man. And your voice is a blessing from God.'

The night was filled with dark shadows. Calls of owls and jackals echoed through the hills. But Jareb didn't notice. He began to sing – not because he was afraid, but because he was happy. He had been brave. He had helped the Saviour.

As Jareb walked, his singing grew louder and stronger. The fearsome noises of the night vanished as owls and jackals fled to distant hills. The only sound the waiting sheep heard that night was Jareb's happy song.

3
Follow that Star!

The Christmas story tells how wise men from the east followed the star to find the baby Jesus and offer him their gifts. Legend turns these mysterious strangers into three kings – Caspar, Melchior and Balthasar. In the stories I have chosen, they represent every race and nation. The last story in the section comes from Australia, and is included specially for younger readers.

Three Kings Came Riding

HENRY WADSWORTH LONGFELLOW

Three Kings came riding from far away,
Melchior and Gaspar and Baltasar;
Three Wise Men out of the East were they,
And they travelled by night and they slept by day,
For their guide was a beautiful, wonderful star.

The star was so beautiful, large and clear,
That all the other stars of the sky
Became a white mist in the atmosphere,
And by this they knew that the coming was near
Of the Prince foretold in the prophecy.

Three caskets they bore on their saddle-bows,
Three caskets of gold with golden keys;
Their robes were of crimson silk, with rows
Of bells and pomegranates and furbelows,
Their turbans like blossoming almond-trees.

And so the Three Kings rode into the West,
Through the dusk of night, over hill and dell,
And sometimes they nodded, with beard on breast,
And sometimes talked, as they paused to rest,
With the people they met at some wayside well.

'Of the child that is born,' said Baltasar,
'Good people, I pray you, tell us the news;
For we in the East have seen his star,
And have ridden fast, and have ridden far,
To find and worship the King of the Jews.'

And the people answered, 'You ask in vain;
We know of no king but Herod the Great!'
They thought the Wise Men were men insane,
As they spurred their horses across the plain,
Like riders in haste, and who cannot wait.

And when they came to Jerusalem,
Herod the Great, who had heard this thing,
Sent for the Wise Men and questioned them;
And said, 'Go down unto Bethlehem,
And bring me tidings of this new king.'

So they rode away; and the star stood still,
The only one in the grey of the morn;
Yes, it stopped, it stood still of its own free will,
Right over Bethlehem on the hill,
The city of David where Christ was born.

And the Three Kings rode through the gate and the guard,
Through the silent street, till their horses turned
And neighed as they entered the great inn-yard;
But the windows were closed, and the doors were barred,
And only a light in the stable burned.

And cradled there in the scented hay,
In the air made sweet by the breath of kine,
The little child in the manger lay,
The child that would be King one day
Of a kingdom not human but divine.

His mother, Mary of Nazareth,
Sat watching beside his place of rest,
Watching the even flow of his breath,
For the joy of life and the terror of death
Were mingled together in her breast.

They laid their offerings at his feet:
The gold was their tribute to a King,
The frankincense, with its odour sweet,
Was for the Priest, the Paraclete,
The myrrh for the body's burying.

And the mother wondered and bowed her head,
And sat as still as a statue of stone;
Her heart was troubled yet comforted,
Remembering what the Angel had said,
Of an endless reign and of David's throne.

Then the Kings rode out of the city gate,
With a clatter of hoofs in proud array;
But they went not back to Herod the Great,
For they knew his malice and feared his hate,
And returned to their homes by another way.

The Journey of the Three

ELIZABETH GIBSON

Once, in far-off lands, there lived three men who were known above all for their wisdom.

One was Caspar, whose eyes snapped blue from the white skin of his face, and whose hair was fair as the snows on the straw roofs of his northern dwelling-place. People who knew Caspar said of him that he was watchful, that his mournful face hid knowledge of secret things. He lived a quiet life, seeing the sun dip only slightly on summer days, and enduring the bitterness of other darker days when the sun rose not at all. By day he loved to climb the crunching cliffs of fjords and watch the circling ascent of eagles; by night he stayed outside when others lapped themselves in fireside warmth, and he watched the stars of the north hang crystals in the bowl of the sky above tiny towns.

The second was Melchior, whose eyes glowed like warm coals from the leathery, red skin of his hawklike face, whose hair was dark and roughened by the savage winds of his steppe home. People who knew Melchior said of him that he was watchful, that his fierce face hid knowledge of things beyond the ordinary. He lived a wild life, fishing with bears for salmon in the furious waters, or riding fast across the flats. By day he was never still, and by night he counted comets as they blazed across the trackless paths of heaven.

The third was Balthasar, whose laughing eyes were black as his woolly hair, and whose smile was like two rows of sweetcorn in the rich earth of his vast farmland. People who knew Balthasar said of him that he was watchful, that his beaming face hid knowledge of things magical and mysterious. He lived a solitary life, herding slow, fat cattle in the deep green wilderness of his southern home. By day he drove the animals to water and pasture, and by night he lit tall fires to frighten wild beasts that would steal his herd; then, beside their flickering light, he would marvel at stars brilliant in nights that fell like cloaks of hot velvet.

These three lived far apart. They lived very different lives. Yet they shared many important things. For all three knew – in the ways of the wise – that earth and sky were made by no man, but that a fathering God reigned over heaven and earth. And that earth was but the mother to mankind; for men were nothing without the Spirit of God. And all three were restless.

Then it was that all three dreamed one night the same strange dream. A Voice whispered to them in the cold wind, the strong wind, the hot wind, that they must make a journey through the world's twisting ways. They must find and follow a star, sharp as a new-hammered sword. And at the end of the long journey they would meet the Child of man, the Child of God. The Voice bade them take nothing with them but their staff, their sandals, and their scrolled maps of heaven and earth, that they might travel swiftly and still be able to track the travelling of the stars, as well as their own ways upon the earth below.

So Caspar turned his back on the frost-painted north. He trained a grey goose to carry him upon her back through the folds of snowy clouds. He lay between her singing wings for many nights and days, flying ever south and east, following the star. In one thing, and in one thing only, Caspar disobeyed the whisper of the cold wind: for he carried with him a gift of gold dug deep from northern mines by dwarves – gold for a King shining with the light of those northern summer days.

So, too, Melchior threw a tapestried blanket over the back of his shrewd pinto pony and rode fleet of foot through the dusty ways of the east, galloping ever west and west, following the star. In one thing and in one thing only, Melchior disobeyed the whisper of the strong wind: for he carried with him a flagon of frankincense, fragrance to waft to the High King of heaven, a sweet savour in the rough places of those endless eastern steppes.

So, also, Balthasar tamed the king of beasts, a cruel-clawed lion, to carry him upon his rippling back through the sun-drenched plains and junglous grasslands, running ever north and east, following the star. In one thing, and in one thing only, Balthasar disobeyed the whisper of the hot wind: for he carried with him a mazer of myrrh, spiced balm to anoint a dying King, brought from the homeland of his heart.

And where were these three travelling? Day and night they journeyed to the place where north met south, where east met west, to a small land forgotten by the people of the earth. A country in the grasp of foreign power, where folk had lost all hope. A country where there was naught for them to do but shepherd sheep upon the sparse hillsides and wait – for something, someone – they scarce knew who.

There, right there in the cross of the continents, these three men stood under the steel of the great star and knew they had arrived. The star's bright blade pierced cloud and cold. It blazed upon a crude cave hewn from solid rock behind an inn, in an unknown village people called 'House of Bread'.

Approaching from the north, the south, the east, they met outside the cave. Each knew the others and why they had come.

Without a word they entered and knelt below the swinging light of a poor lantern, among the stink of animals, where no king should be born but this One. A woman was there, a young woman with a tired face and tranquil eyes, and an old man, who bowed and offered them bread and wine to comfort them after their long travelling.

Above the cave the star hung ruthless as a rending sword, fit to break the heart of the quiet woman and her husband. Then these three men of wisdom knew that this was no ordinary child, and that their coming had been right in the eyes of heaven's Maker.

In turn they bowed themselves before the outstretched, babish fingers of the Infant in the straw: those same fingers that had sprinkled stars upon heaven's highways, scattered snow upon the mountains, and planted grass upon the plains. And their wisdom told them that although this was the end of their old lives, it was also a wondrous beginning.

Caspar and the Star

FRANCESCA BOSCA, TRANSLATED BY PHILIP HAWTHORN

Caspar was a wise and clever man who lived in a tiny house perched on the top of a hill.

Every night he could be seen gazing up at the sky, for the study of the stars was the love of his life.

As soon as the first stars appeared in the evening sky, Caspar would hurry outside and gaze at them in wide-eyed wonder.

During the day Caspar would read book after book, only lifting his head to watch for the darkening of the evening sky. Then he would smile – sitting by the window, waiting amid the silence of a thousand thoughts.

Then suddenly, one evening, the silence was broken: 'It's here! It's come! At last the star has arrived!'

Shouting and waving his arms above his head, Caspar ran outside, bursting with joy. The star for which he had been waiting so long was there right in front of him – and it was more beautiful and majestic than any star he had ever seen before.

He decided that he must begin his journey at once. So, packing everything he needed, he left his house and set off. He wouldn't need a map: this special star would show him the way – the way to a very special baby.

Caspar followed the star for many nights until he found himself in front of the most wonderful palace. It had hundreds of turrets, and the walls were covered with glittering jewels.

He stopped and stared in amazement: the palace was so resplendent that it lit up the dark night sky.

The star had also stopped, and so Caspar thought that he had reached the end of his journey.

Next morning, inside the palace, Caspar met a man called Melchior. He also loved to study the stars and the two men were soon talking like old friends. Caspar told him all about his journey and the star that he was following.

Smiling broadly, Melchior replied: 'I also am here to look for the baby, and I think I have found him. Someone told me that a few days ago the queen gave birth to her first son. Perhaps this is the baby for whom we are searching!'

Together they went to the royal court and asked if they could see the baby.

As they entered the room, Caspar's heart began to beat faster.

'Do you remember what the ancient books told us?' he whispered. 'He is the one who will bring joy and peace to all the world. He will comfort the poor and the sad – and kings and queens will bow down before him.'

'Yes, this must be him,' replied Melchior.

But they were wrong. For just then, something in the sky caught their eye: it was the star, moving away from the palace.

So Caspar and Melchior set off on their journey once more, faithfully following the star. After a few days it stopped again, having led them to a city that was so beautiful, the two friends were left absolutely speechless.

But this was no time for sightseeing – they hurried off in search of the baby. Inside the king's palace they met a man called Balthazar, and they told him all about their adventure.

'You won't believe it,' replied Balthazar, 'but I've been following the star as well! I also want to find this baby – my books have spoken so much about him.' Then he lowered his voice and continued with great excitement: 'I've heard that the king and queen here have recently had a son – let's go and see him!'

As they looked at the baby, Melchior remembered what his books had promised: 'He will be a great king. He will bring his people out of the land of darkness into the kingdom of light.'

'Just look at him, surely he is our king!' exclaimed Balthazar.

But once more the star had begun to move on its continuing journey.

At once the three wise men also left the city and followed the way that the star showed them.

But now their faces were full of sadness. Maybe their books had not told the truth, or maybe this star was not the one they were supposed to follow?

The three wise men rode along in silence for mile after weary mile, each of them wrapped up in his own thoughts.

Soon they noticed that even the star had abandoned them: it' had suddenly disappeared. Now their troubled hearts became even heavier with doubts and questions.

'Maybe the time has come for us to turn back,' sighed Caspar, with bitter disappointment.

But just at that moment Balthazar interrupted him.

'Look, you two! I can see lights – down there!' he said, pointing excitedly. 'It's a city! Perhaps we'll find someone there who can give us some answers.'

Their hopes rose again as they approached the city of Jerusalem.

The following day, news of the three strangers reached the court of King Herod, a powerful and cruel man. Herod was very worried by what he heard, so he brought together all his advisers.

'There are three men in the city asking about the birth of a baby,' he said, frowning. 'They say he will be king of all people. What does all this mean – who is this baby?'

Herod's advisers could only confirm his fears: their books also told about the coming of a very special baby. But Herod would not listen to them.

'I am the only king around here!' he boomed, 'and I will protect my throne at all costs – even if I have to kill to do it!'

Herod banged his fist down, almost cracking his throne. Then he smiled, and said: 'Invite these strangers to the palace. I'd like a little chat with them.'

Caspar, Melchior and Balthazar gladly accepted Herod's invitation; at last someone might be able to help them. However, once they were standing in front of him, their enthusiasm gradually began to trickle away. Herod gave no answers at all, he only asked question after question. He asked them about each and every detail of their journey and what they hoped to find.

As he wished them farewell, he said: 'Go and search for the baby, and when you have found him, let me know so that I can also go and... worship him!'

The three wise men left the palace, very disturbed by this strange meeting. Herod did not seem to be as happy or excited about the baby's coming as they were. What did he really want?

That evening, feeling puzzled and confused, the three wise men left Jerusalem. Then, after journeying for many cold, dark hours, they saw the faint glow of a small fire in the middle of a clearing.

As they drew nearer they noticed, seated near the fire, a shepherd who was keeping a watch on his flock. Without hesitation he invited the three strangers to sit down and warm themselves.

Caspar, Melchior and Balthazar told the shepherd the story of their long journey. He thought for a moment, then said: 'The other day I came upon a strange sight. At Bethlehem, it was. A couple with a tiny baby – just been born, he had – and they'd put him in a manger. Someone said he was a king! Well, there were no armies or servants around him, but even so his little face made me so happy and... peaceful. I felt special just to be there.'

The three wise men looked at each other, then they eagerly asked the shepherd to take them to the place and show them this baby. Along the way the star appeared once more, shining more brightly than ever – just like the hope in their hearts.

When they arrived, Caspar, Melchior and Balthazar knelt down beside the baby. They tingled with a new joy that made them want to stay and worship him for ever.

At last they had found the King of Love – and their real journey had just begun.

Carol of the Brown King

LANGSTON HUGHES

Of the three Wise Men
Who came to the King,
One was a brown man,
So they sing.

Of the three Wise Men
Who followed the Star,
One was a brown king
From afar.

They brought fine gifts
Of spices and gold
In jewelled boxes
Of beauty untold.

Unto His humble
Manger they came
And bowed their heads
In Jesus' name.

Three Wise Men,
One dark like me –
Part of His
Nativity.

The Three Wise Men

ALISON UTTLEY

One Christmas Eve, during a heavy snowstorm, a man and his young wife sat talking by the fire. They lived in a lonely little cottage beyond the village, and there were many days when they saw nobody. That did not prevent the wife from being merry and cheerful, but the husband often wished for company.

'Last year we went to Cousin Goodman's for Christmas Eve, but we can't go anywhere tonight,' he grumbled. 'Hark to the gale out there! How wild it is!'

The wind howled like a wolf and the trees howled back. The door latch rattled, as if somebody were touching it. The snow swept up in drifts across the garden, and piled itself high against the walls.

'It's a bad storm. Nobody could go out on a wild blustery night like this,' agreed the wife. 'I'm thankful we have a good roof over our heads, Simon.'

'Aye. We've a lot to be thankful for, I suppose,' Simon answered gloomily. Mary threw a fresh log on the fire, so that the flames danced in the chimney and showers of sparks made a little fountain like the fireworks on Guy Fawkes' day. It was a cheerful sight, she thought, to see the yellow flames and the gold caves in the fire. She fetched some apples from the larder and put them in a tin in the oven by the fireside to bake for supper. She spread the blue and white cloth on the table, and brought out the Sunday plates and mugs.

'It's Christmas Eve, and a feast night,' said she. 'We always have our best china on this night.'

There was cream from their own cow, Strawberry, next door in the little cowplace. Mary set it on the table in the old silver jug. Even as she paused to polish the jug, she could hear the rattle of the chain and the thud of the cow's body against the dividing wall. She put some milk on the fire to warm for the Christmas Eve posset, and added cloves and a dash of ale to it for her husband.

55

'Now I'll make our Christmas Eve posset. You'll like that, won't you?' she said. She lifted down the posset mug from the mantelpiece while her husband watched her. There was a candle burning on the mantelpiece, shining out over the little room, and as it was Christmas Eve she lighted another and placed it in its polished brass candlestick on the table.

'Aren't we grand tonight?' she laughed. 'We might be expecting company, so fine we are. When I was little, it was Santa Claus himself who came round on this night, and weren't we excited! I do love Christmas Eve.'

She smoothed her hair in front of the little glass on the wall, and she put on a clean linen apron and her mother's gold brooch. 'There,' she said, 'now I'm ready for the king himself.'

Her husband only stared at the fire. His young wife was always making little jokes, to wheedle a smile to his face. He was anxious and poor and worried about small things.

'It does look nice, Simon, doesn't it?' she asked, kneeling at his side for a moment.

He looked at her sweet face turned to his, and stroked her hair. 'It's lovely, Mary. You've made it grand. I've never seen it so nice before. You can make a feast when there's an empty pantry. You make everything pretty you handle.'

She leaped to her feet with joy at his words, and danced round the room, putting the final touches to the holly and ivy that decked the walls. Along the edge of the stone mantelpiece hung a chain of scarlet berries which she had threaded that afternoon, and in each brass pitcher and pan she stuck a spray of greenery.

There were not many pictures in the little room – a wool-work embroidered picture of Christ blessing the children, a cross-stitch sampler, and a painting of a cart-horse. Round the frames she had twisted garlands of holly and sprays of ivy, and sprigs of berries decked the looking-glass and the dresser.

From the middle of the ceiling hung the Kissing-bunch. It was a large bunch of holly with the choicest berries, all trimmed neatly into a round smooth ball of greenery. It was suspended by a string from a hook, and underneath it a visitor must take a kiss. Such was the custom of those times, when Christmas trees were hardly known.

'It's as lovely a Kissing-bunch as ever I remember,' said Simon, gazing up at it. The ball glittered in the firelight. The rosy apples

and yellow oranges hanging in the bunch gleamed, and the silver bells, gilded walnuts and little flags of paper stuck in the Kissing-bunch made a brightness that seemed to shine out like a lamp.

Simon rose to his full height and drawing his little wife close to him he kissed her under the prickly bunch. 'Thank you for making so many pleasures out of nothing,' said he.

At that moment, as they stood there with the Kissing-bunch dangling above their heads, there was a loud thud at the door, and the wind cried more fiercely than ever. They both looked in surprise. The door was locked with the great old key, and bolted with iron bolts, and a mat lay at the bottom to keep the room warm.

'What's that?' asked Mary. 'Is somebody there?'

'Only the wind, my dear,' Simon replied, and pushed the door mat closer.

Again came the thump like a knock on the door.

'Who is it?' asked Mary.

'We'll soon see,' Simon answered, and he drew the bolts and unlocked the door.

Yes, there was somebody there, out in the deep snow. An ancient man stood in the shadows by the cowplace. He didn't speak. He was white with snow, as if he had walked far in it. His back was bowed, but one could see that he was very tall. He leaned on a crooked staff.

'Come in out of the storm,' said Simon. 'What are you doing here at this time of night? Come in, come in, master.'

The old man stepped into the room. He took no notice of Simon and Mary, but he looked round eagerly as if he were seeking

57

somebody. The two stared at him in astonishment. His face was dark-skinned, and wrinkled in a thousand creases, but it had a noble expression, serene and wise. His eyes glittered like stars with emotion as he saw the Kissing-bunch. His clothes were of a strange fashion, worn and old, stained and tattered. On his shoulders was a cloak, white with its covering of snow.

'Who are you, and what do you want?' asked Simon again, but he hesitated as he spoke, for it seemed rude to question such a traveller as this.

'My name is Balthazar, and I am looking for Him,' said the old man, very slowly, and his voice rang through the room like a deep bell.

Mary put her warm young hand on the crooked fingers that clasped the staff, gently released their grasp, and put the staff in the corner.

'Poor old man, you're as cold as ice,' she said. 'Come here and sit by the fire and warm yourself. Make yourself at home, for it's Christmas Eve, and we're glad to have you. There's nobody but just ourselves, so stay the night. We can't turn you out to look for that friend you were talking about. Stay here; bide with us and share our Christmas Eve supper.'

As he turned his intent gaze upon her, Mary was filled with sudden happiness. She poured out warm water for him to wash at the sink. She gave him a towel to dry himself, and she hung up his cloak on the hook behind the door.

'Sit you here,' said she, drawing the Windsor armchair up to the table. 'There's roast apples and mince-pies, and a hot posset to drink.'

She fetched another mug and plate and made ready for him. He murmured his gratitude to her. Before he ate, he folded his hands together, and said a prayer in a foreign tongue. Mary and Simon had their supper with him, waiting on him and serving him, but they did not bother him with questions. When he had finished he sat quietly by the fire.

'You can sleep here, in the kitchen, where it is warm,' said Simon.

'Thank you,' said the old man, 'I shall not sleep, but I shall be glad to wait here for Him. This is a beautiful home.'

Mary smiled happily and nodded at the Kissing-bunch.

'You like my Kissing-bunch?' she said.

'It is a holy thing. This is the kind of place where He might come,' the old man said, simply, and he looked at the bunch of holly as if he could see more than was visible to their eyes.

'Sing your Christmas Eve carol, Mary,' said Simon. 'I am sure our visitor will like it. You always sing it at Christmas!' So Mary, shy before the stranger, sang in a small sweet voice, and Simon played his fiddle to accompany her.

Silent night! Holy night!
All is calm, all is bright;
Round yon Virgin Mother and Child
Holy infant so tender and mild,
Sleep in heavenly peace.
Sleep in heavenly peace.

They said good night and went upstairs, with a backward glance at their strange guest. He sat by the fire, but his head was turned to the Kissing-bunch, and he seemed to be waiting and listening for something.

In the night Mary was wakened by music coming out of the air, filling the whole cottage with exquisite sound. It floated round her and she lay enchanted, listening. It was a high clear tune, like the wind makes, but many flutes seemed to be playing at once.

Sweet and low it went, and then high, ringing through the room.

'Hark! Simon,' she whispered, nudging her husband. 'Listen to that music. Where does it come from?'

Simon sat up. 'It's all around us, Mary,' said he. 'Is it the old man playing something downstairs? Let's go and see.'

'He couldn't play like that, Simon. It's a lot of people playing. Just listen to it.'

They crept softly down the creaking stairs and opened the kitchen door. A golden glow filled the room with radiance and they saw a wonderful sight. There were three men there, and although they recognized the old traveller among them, he was changed. The men were dressed in royal Eastern robes, golden and scarlet and white. They were kneeling on the stone floor with their heads bowed and their arms stretched out holding gifts.

The tall, dark old man, Balthazar, held sweet-smelling myrrh, and the fragrance of it filled the little kitchen. His scarlet cloak, sprinkled with stars, was spread out around him.

Another man, with a long grey beard, held in his hands a lump of gleaming gold. His blue cloak was wrapped closely to him, and his face was hidden.

The third, a young man, had taken off a gold crown which lay near him. His white cloak was like the snow outside. He offered the gift of frankincense, which burned like incense.

The three men knelt towards a light which came from no earthly candle or flame or fire. Under the Kissing-bunch was a heap of yellow straw from the shed next door, and on it lay the Baby. The Child was laughing at the Kissing-bunch and looking up at it. Over him leaned His Mother, her cloak flowing to the ground, her arms encircling the Holy Child.

The music got louder, voices were now singing, but whether it was really the wind in the bare trees, or angels in the sky, Simon and Mary did not know, for nobody was visible. The music filled the room, the air was sweet-scented and the scarlet berries on the Kissing-bunch gleamed like a thousand candles. The little Child stretched out His fingers towards an apple and a gilded walnut, and He laughed into His Mother's eyes, as she smiled down at him.

Simon and Mary knelt in the doorway, and even as they looked at the Baby, the light dimmed, and the music became faint. Shadows crept from the corners and the vision faded away. There was only the flickering dying fire which shone on the old man, kneeling under the Kissing-bunch in his dark, soiled clothes.

They closed the door and went upstairs to talk of what they had seen.

'It was the Child Jesus and His Mother and the Three Wise Men,' whispered Mary.

'I remember a tale I heard from my grandmother,' said Simon. 'I had forgotten it till now. There's an old legend that the Three Wise Men every Christmas seek for the Holy Child. They travel from land to land in any Christian country to find the place where He might come, and when they have chosen, they enter, and the Miracle of the first Christmas happens again.'

'Who is the old man downstairs?' asked Mary.

'He is Balthazar, and he goes ahead to find the cottage that is swept and clean all ready for the guests.'

'And the others?' asked Mary. 'Who was that with the crown?'

'That was Caspar, King of Chaldea, and the grey-bearded one Melchior, King of Nubia. But I am very tired, Mary. I feel dazed and strange. My eyes won't stay open and I must sleep.'

Simon dropped on the bed and was fast asleep in a moment, and Mary too was soon lost in dreams.

It was dawn on Christmas Day when they awoke, and at once they went downstairs, hurrying to see the old man, to ask him about the vision. There was no trace of him, not a clot of melting snow on the floor, or a mark of a footstep. Only, hanging in the Kissing-bunch were three little boxes of cedar wood, sweetly perfumed and delicately made. They dangled in the green leaves among the apples and oranges, the gilded walnuts and the silver bells.

'Look!' cried Mary. 'Those were not there last night. Who left them there? Was it the old man – or those others who came?'

'Those others,' said Simon, thoughtfully.

The boxes hung by thin woven grass strings, and he untied the knots and took them down. They were smooth as silk, rare and beautiful, carved from the golden wood. He turned them over, and they flew open to show their treasures. In one was a lump of yellow gold, in another myrrh and in the third an ointment made from frankincense.

'The Three Wise Men have left part of their offering here to remind us of their visit for always,' said Mary.

'We shall never forget this happening,' agreed Simon. 'We will always prepare for the Holy Child on Christmas Eve.'

The next year was a time of prosperity for them, and everything went well. At Christmas a baby had come to share their home and their love. They swept the hearth on Christmas Eve, and hung up the Kissing-bunch, but the Three Wise Men were far away. Their own little child held up his tiny hands to the berries and apples and oranges, and the light seemed to shine down upon him when Mary sang her carol.

Later, when he was old enough to understand, they showed him the three little boxes which the Three Wise Men had brought, and they told him this story of the coming of the Christ Child.

Kippy Koala's Christmas Present

WIN MORGAN

The afternoon sun slipped behind the hilltop, sending rays of golden arrows between the tall white eucalyptus trees. The grey-green leaves and the pale yellow blossoms moved in the gentle breeze. It was nearly Christmas.

High in the fork of his favourite gum tree sat Kippy Koala. He watched contentedly as the shadows lengthened and the last golden glow faded to pink and blue.

The gleam of the first star of the evening caught Kippy's eye. It hung low in the sky, twinkling above the dark treetops. What a bright white light it was!

Kippy sat up straight, eyes wide open now, trying hard to remember something Uncle Wainwright Wombat had told him. It was a story about some Wise Men who had followed a bright star a long time ago.

'Now why did they follow that star?' he wondered, frowning hard and scratching his tummy in an effort to remember.

Soon the night animals emerged from the hollows where they had been sleeping through the long summer day. They sniffed and scratched, searching for their supper under the dried leaves and fallen trees.

Suddenly, with a flurry of wings, Mother Owl landed beside Kippy. She fluffed her tawny feathers and stared at him in surprise.

'It's past sunset, Kippy. Why aren't you gathering your supper?'

Fixing his brown eyes on Mother Owl, Kippy asked in a puzzled voice, 'Why did the Wise Men follow the star a long time ago?'

'Hoo, hoo,' hooted Mother Owl softly. 'You do have a bad memory. That's part of the Christmas story. When the Wise Men saw the star, they knew a great king had been born. And that king was the baby Jesus.'

Kippy's eyes shone. 'Yes, now I remember. They brought special gifts to the baby king. Oh, I wish I could have brought a present to him.'

'Well,' said Mother Owl, 'giving presents to others is like giving presents to Jesus.'

Kippy blinked. 'Like taking a present to the little baby at the log hut,' he added, half to himself.

Without another word, Kippy Koala had scrambled out to the end of the branch and reached for the tenderest gum-tips. Gathering as many as he could carry, he backed down the tall tree.

Peering up through the dark treetops, Kippy saw the bright evening star. Smiling to himself, he set off along the track: through the ferns and heath, down the hillside and along the creek bank where Uncle Wainwright Wombat lived.

'Where are you going, Kippy?' called Uncle Wainwright.

'I'm taking a special gift to the baby,' he answered. Before Uncle Wainwright could ask any more questions, he padded across the creek and disappeared into the shadows.

It was very dark. As he stumbled over hidden roots and rocks Kippy could hear the night animals whispering and scratching in the undergrowth. The trees, scrub and rocks formed strange shapes in the shadows. They seemed to close around him then step back as he pushed past.

A wallaby suddenly appeared out of the darkness ahead. Startled, it leapt and bounded down the slope into the night, scattering twigs and crashing through the undergrowth. Then all was still. Kippy had never been this far from his favourite gum tree before. He didn't feel quite so brave now.

Kippy picked his way carefully along the narrow track, clutching his bunch of tender gum-tips. The deep shadows of the bush gave way to a grassy clearing. Kippy stood still, searching for that bright star. Many more stars were twinkling now and they lit up a rough log hut with smoke wisping from the chimney and a yellow light gleaming in the window.

Softly he padded towards the door and, and standing in the shadow, peered in.

The glowing coals of a friendly fire lit up the stone chimney and iron roof. A battered lamp, standing on a rough bush table, shed a soft circle of light. Kippy gazed in wonder at a mother gently rocking her baby.

Kippy Koala quietly placed the bunch of tender gum-tips on the step of the rough hut. This was the best gift he could give. With one last look at the mother and baby, he turned and padded slowly back through the tall trees. He was not afraid of the whisperings and scratchings now, and he smiled as he thought of the lonely bush mother and her tiny child – and the gift he had given.

As he crossed the creek, Uncle Wainwright Wombat called to him, 'Did you find the baby?' Kippy climbed up the creek bank and sat down contentedly next to Uncle Wainwright. Lifting his eyes, he searched for the star. Yes, there it was, shining brightly.

Kippy thought about the mother rocking her baby beside the fire, the lamplight falling softly on their faces.

'Yes, Uncle, I found the baby and I gave him the very best gift I could.'

Uncle Wainwright smiled gently and began once more to tell Kippy Koala the story of the very first Christmas.

4
Timeless Stories

Some Christmas stories have become specially well-known down the years. All of those included in this section are by famous authors.

Everyone knows old Scrooge the miser from Charles Dickens' *A Christmas Carol*. Hans Christian Andersen's *The Little Match Girl* is a sad story; it makes us think about children in need. In *Little Women* Mrs March's girls discover the cost – and the rewards – of loving their neighbour at Christmas time. And no collection would be complete without something from C.S. Lewis' Narnia stories.

Papa Panov's Special Christmas

From *The Complete Works of Leo Tolstoy*

RETOLD BY MARY BATCHELOR

It was Christmas Eve and although it was still afternoon, lights had begun to appear in the shops and houses of the little Russian village, for the short winter day was nearly over. Excited children scurried indoors and now only muffled sounds of chatter and laughter escaped the closed shutters.

Old Papa Panov, the village shoemaker, stepped outside his shop to take one last look around. The sounds of happiness, the bright lights and the faint but delicious smells of Christmas cooking reminded him of past Christmas times when his wife had been alive and his own children little. Now they had gone. His usually cheerful face, with the little laughter wrinkles behind the round steel spectacles, looked sad now. But he went back indoors with a firm step, put up the shutters and set a pot of coffee to heat on the charcoal stove. Then, with a sigh, he settled in his big armchair.

Papa Panov did not often read, but tonight he pulled down the big old family Bible and, slowly tracing the lines with one finger, he read again the Christmas story. He read how Mary and Joseph, tired by their journey to Bethlehem, found no room for them at the inn, so that Mary's little baby was born in the cowshed.

'Oh dear, oh dear!' exclaimed Papa Panov. 'If only they had come here! I would have given them my bed and I could have covered the baby with my patchwork quilt to keep him warm.'

He read on about the Wise Men who had come to see the baby Jesus, bringing him splendid gifts. Papa Panov's face fell.

'I have no gift that I could give him,' he thought sadly.

Then his face brightened. He put down the Bible, got up and stretched his long arms to the shelf high up in his little room. He took down a small, dusty box and opened it. Inside was a perfect pair of tiny leather shoes. Papa Panov smiled with satisfaction. Yes, they were as good as he had remembered – the best shoes he had ever made.

'I should give him those,' he decided as he gently put them away and sat down again.

He was feeling tired now, and the further he read the sleepier he became. The print began to dance before his eyes so that he closed them, just for a moment. In no time at all Papa Panov was fast asleep.

And as he slept he dreamed. He dreamed that someone was in his room and he knew at once, as one does in dreams, who the person was. It was Jesus.

'You have been wishing that you could see me, Papa Panov,' he said kindly, 'then look for me tomorrow. It will be Christmas Day and I will visit you. But look carefully, for I shall not tell you who I am.'

When at last Papa Panov awoke, the bells were ringing out and a thin light was filtering through the shutters.

'Bless my soul!' said Papa Panov. 'It's Christmas Day!'

He stood up and stretched himself for he was rather stiff. Then his face filled with happiness as he remembered his dream. This would be a very special Christmas after all, for Jesus was coming to visit. How would he look? Would he be a little baby, as at that first Christmas? Would he be a grown man, a carpenter – or the great King that he is, God's Son? He must watch carefully the whole day through so that he recognized him however he came.

Papa Panov put on a special pot of coffee for his Christmas breakfast, took down the shutters and looked out of the window. The street was deserted, no one was stirring yet. No one except the road sweeper. He looked as miserable and dirty as ever, and well he might! Whoever wanted to work on Christmas Day – and in the raw cold and bitter freezing mist of such a morning?

Papa Panov opened the shop door, letting in a thin stream of cold air. 'Come in!' he shouted across the street cheerily. 'Come and have some hot coffee to keep out the cold!'

The sweeper looked up, scarcely able to believe his ears. He was only too glad to put down his broom and come into the warm room. His old clothes steamed gently in the heat of the stove and he clasped both red hands round the comforting warm mug as he drank.

Papa Panov watched him with satisfaction, but every now and then his eyes strayed to the window. It would never do to miss his special visitor.

'Expecting someone?' the sweeper asked at last. So Papa Panov told him about his dream. 'Well, I hope he comes,' the sweeper said, 'you've given me a bit of Christmas cheer I never expected to have. I'd say you deserve to have your dream come true.' And he actually smiled.

When he had gone, Papa Panov put on cabbage soup for his dinner, then went to the door again, scanning the street. He saw no one. But he was mistaken. Someone *was* coming.

The girl walked so slowly and quietly, hugging the walls of shops and houses, that it was a while before he noticed her. She looked very tired and she was carrying something. As she drew nearer he could see that it was a baby, wrapped in a thin shawl. There was such sadness in her face and in the pinched little face of the baby, that Papa Panov's heart went out to them.

'Won't you come in?' he called, stepping outside to meet them. 'You both need a warm by the fire and a rest.'

The young mother let him shepherd her indoors and to the comfort of the armchair. She gave a big sigh of relief.

'I'll warm some milk for the baby,' Papa Panov said, 'I've had children of my own – I can feed her for you.' He took the milk from the stove and carefully fed the baby from a spoon, warming her tiny feet by the stove at the same time.

'She needs shoes,' the cobbler said.

But the girl replied, 'I can't afford shoes, I've got no husband to bring home money. I'm on my way to the next village to get work.'

A sudden thought flashed into Papa Panov's mind. He remembered the little shoes he had looked at last night. But he had been keeping those for Jesus. He looked again at the cold little feet and made up his mind.

'Try these on her,' he said, handing the baby and the shoes to the mother. The beautiful little shoes were a perfect fit. The girl smiled happily and the baby gurgled with pleasure.

'You have been so kind to us,' the girl said, when she got up with her baby to go. 'May all your Christmas wishes come true!'

But Papa Panov was beginning to wonder if his very special Christmas wish *would* come true. Perhaps he had missed his visitor? He looked anxiously up and down the street. There were plenty of people about but they were all faces that he recognized. There were neighbours going to call on their families. They nodded and smiled and wished him Happy Christmas! Or beggars – and Papa Panov hurried indoors to fetch them hot soup and a generous hunk of bread, hurrying out again in case he missed the Important Stranger.

All too soon the winter dusk fell. When Papa Panov next went to the door and strained his eyes he could no longer make out the passers-by. Most were home and indoors by now anyway. He walked slowly back into his room at last, put up the shutters and sat down wearily in his armchair.

So it has been just a dream after all.

Jesus had not come.

Then all at once he knew that he was no longer alone in the room.

This was no dream for he was wide awake. At first he seemed to see before his eyes the long stream of people who had come to him that day. He saw again the old road sweeper, the young mother and her baby and the beggars he had fed. As they passed, each whispered, 'Didn't you see *me*, Papa Panov?'

'Who are you?' he called out, bewildered.

Then another voice answered him. It was the voice from his dream – the voice of Jesus.

'I was hungry and you fed me,' he said. 'I was naked and you clothed me. I was cold and you warmed me. I came to you today in every one of those you helped and welcomed.'

Then all was quiet and still. Only the sound of the big clock ticking. A great peace and happiness seemed to fill the room, over-flowing Papa Panov's heart until he wanted to burst out singing and laughing and dancing with joy.

'So he *did* come after all!' was all that he said.

Old Scrooge – and Tiny Tim

From *A Christmas Carol*

CHARLES DICKENS

Once upon a time – of all the good days in the year, on Christmas Eve – old Scrooge sat busy in his counting house. It was cold, bleak, biting weather: foggy withal: and he could hear the people in the court outside go wheezing up and down, beating their hands upon their breasts, and stamping their feet upon the pavement-stones to warm them. The city clocks had only just gone three, but it was quite dark already: it had not been light all day: and candles were flaring in the windows of the neighbouring offices, like ruddy smears upon the palpable brown air. The fog came pouring in at every chink and keyhole, and was so dense without, that although the court was of the narrowest, the houses opposite were mere phantoms.

The door of Scrooge's counting-house was open that he might keep his eye upon his clerk, Bob Cratchit, who in a dismal little cell beyond, a sort of tank, was copying letters. Scrooge had a very small fire, but the clerk's fire was so very much smaller that it looked like one coal. But he couldn't replenish it, for Scrooge kept the coal-box in his own room... Wherefore the clerk put on his white comforter, and tried to warm himself at the candle; in which effort, not being a man of a strong imagination, he failed.

'A merry Christmas, uncle! God save you!' cried a cheerful voice. It was the voice of Scrooge's nephew, who came upon him so quickly that this was the first intimation he had of his approach.

'Bah!' said Scrooge. 'Humbug!'

He had so heated himself with rapid walking in the fog and frost, this nephew of Scrooge's, that he was all in a glow; his face was ruddy and handsome; his eyes sparkled, and his breath smoked again.

'Christmas a humbug, uncle!' said Scrooge's nephew. 'You don't mean that, I am sure.'

'I do,' said Scrooge. 'Merry Christmas! What right have you to be merry? What reason have you to be merry? You're poor enough.'

'Come, then,' returned the nephew gaily. 'What right have you to be dismal? What reason have you to be morose? You're rich enough.'

Scrooge having no better answer ready on the spur of the moment, said, 'Bah!' again; and followed it up with 'Humbug.'

'Don't be cross, uncle,' said the nephew.

'What else can I be,' returned the uncle, 'when I live in such a world of fools as this Merry Christmas! Out upon merry Christmas. What's Christmas time to you but a time for paying bills without money; a time for finding yourself a year older, and not an hour richer..? If I could work my will,' said Scrooge, indignantly, 'every idiot who goes about with "Merry Christmas," on his lips, should be boiled with his own pudding, and buried with a stake of holly through his heart. He should!'

'Uncle!' pleaded the nephew.

'Nephew!' returned the uncle, sternly, 'Keep Christmas in your own way, and let me keep it in mine.'

'Keep it!' repeated Scrooge's nephew. 'But you don't keep it.'

'Let me leave it alone, then,' said Scrooge. 'Much good may it do you! Much good it has ever done you!'

'There are many things from which I might have derived good, by which I have not profited, I dare say,' returned the nephew: 'Christmas among the rest. But I am sure I have always thought of Christmas time, when it has come round – apart from the veneration due to its sacred name and origin, if anything belonging to it can be apart from that – as a good time: a kind, forgiving, charitable, pleasant time: the only time I know of, in the long calendar of the year, when men and women seem by one consent to open their shut-up hearts freely, and to think of people below them as if they really were fellow-passengers to the grave, and not another race of creatures bound on other journeys. And therefore, uncle, though it has never put a scrap of gold or silver in my pocket, I believe that it *has* done me good, and *will* do me good: and I say, God bless it!'

Despite his nephew's best efforts, old Scrooge seems totally set in his mean and miserly ways. But three ghostly visitors – the Ghost of Christmas Past, the Ghost of Christmas Present, and the Ghost of Christmas Future – are about to give him a shock. We enter the home of Scrooge's clerk, Bob Cratchit, for their family Christmas. Unseen, Scrooge, with the Ghost of Christmas Present, looks on ...

'What has ever got your precious father then,' said Mrs Cratchit. 'And your brother, Tiny Tim! And Martha, warn't as late last Christmas Day by half-an-hour!'

'Here's Martha, mother!' said a girl, appearing as she spoke.

'Here's Martha, mother!' cried the two young Cratchits. 'Hurrah! There's such a goose, Martha!'

'Why, bless your heart alive, my dear, how late you are!' said Mrs Cratchit, kissing her a dozen times, and taking off her shawl and bonnet for her with officious zeal.

'We'd a deal of work to finish up last night,' replied the girl, 'and had to clear away this morning, mother!'

'Well! Never mind so long as you are come,' said Mrs Cratchit. 'Sit ye down before the fire, my dear, and have a warm, Lord bless ye!'

'No, no! There's father coming,' cried the two young Cratchits, who were everywhere at once. 'Hide, Martha, hide!' So Martha hid herself, and in came little Bob, the father, with at least three feet of comforter exclusive of the fringe, hanging down before him; and his thread-bare clothes darned up and brushed, to look seasonable: and Tiny Tim upon his shoulder. Alas for Tiny Tim, he bore a little crutch, and had his limbs supported by an iron frame!

'Why, where's our Martha?' cried Bob Cratchit looking round.

'Not coming,' said Mrs Cratchit.

'Not coming!' said Bob, with a sudden declension in his high spirits; for he had been Tim's blood horse all the way from church, and had come home rampant. 'Not coming on Christmas Day!'

Martha didn't like to see him disappointed, if it were only in joke; so she came out prematurely from behind the closet door, and ran into his arms, while the two young Cratchits hustled Tiny Tim, and bore him off into the wash-house that he might hear the pudding singing in the copper.

'And how did little Tim behave?' asked Mrs Cratchit, when she had rallied Bob on his credulity and Bob had hugged his daughter to his heart's content.

'As good as gold,' said Bob, 'and better. Somehow he gets thoughtful, sitting by himself so much, and thinks the strangest things you ever heard. He told me, coming home, that he hoped the people saw him in the church, because he was a cripple, and it might be pleasant to them to remember on Christmas Day, who made lame beggars walk and blind men see.'

Bob's voice was tremulous when he told them this, and trembled more when he said that Tiny Tim was growing strong and hearty.

His active little crutch was heard upon the floor, and back came Tiny Tim before another word was spoken, escorted by his brother and sister to his stool beside the fire; and while Bob, turning up his cuffs – as if, poor fellow, they were capable of being made more shabby – compounded some hot mixture in a jug with gin and lemons, and stirred it round and round and put it on the hob to simmer; Master Peter and the two ubiquitous young Cratchits went to fetch the goose, with which they soon returned in high procession.

Such a bustle ensued that you might have thought a goose the rarest of birds; a feathered phenomenon, to which a black swan was a matter of course; and in truth it was something very like it in that house. Mrs Cratchit made the gravy (ready beforehand in a little saucepan) hissing hot; Master Peter mashed the potatoes with incredible vigour; Miss Belinda sweetened up the apple-sauce; Martha dusted the hot plates; Bob took Tiny Tim beside him in a tiny corner at the table; the two young Crachits set chairs for everybody, not forgetting themselves, and mounting guard upon their posts, crammed spoons into their mouths, lest they should shriek for goose before their turn came to be helped. At last the dishes were set on, and grace was said. It was succeeded by a breathless pause, as Mrs Cratchit, looking slowly all along the carving-knife, prepared to plunge it in the breast; but when she did, and when the long expected gush of stuffing issued forth, one murmur of delight arose all round the board, and even Tiny Tim, excited by the two young Cratchits, beat on the table with the handle of his knife, and feebly cried Hurrah!

There never was such a goose. Bob said he didn't believe there ever was such a goose cooked. Its tenderness and flavour, size and cheapness, were the themes of universal admiration. Eked out by the apple-sauce and mashed potatoes, it was a sufficient dinner for the whole family; indeed, as Mrs Cratchit said with great delight (surveying one small atom of bone upon the dish), they hadn't ate it all at last! Yet every one had had enough, and the youngest Cratchits in particular, were steeped in sage and onion to the eyebrows! But now, the plates being changed by Miss Belinda, Mrs Cratchit left the room alone – too nervous to bear witnesses – to take the pudding up, and bring it in.

Suppose it should not be done enough! Suppose it should break in turning out! Suppose somebody should have got over the wall of the back-yard, and stolen it, while they were merry with the goose; a supposition at which the two young Cratchits became livid! All sorts of horrors were supposed.

Hallo! A great deal of steam! The pudding was out of the copper. A smell like a washing-day! That was the cloth. A smell like an eating-house, and a pastry cook's next door to each other, with a laundress's next door to that! That was the pudding. In half a minute Mrs Cratchit entered: flushed, but smiling proudly; with the pudding, like a speckled cannon-ball, so hard and firm, blazing in half of half-a-quartern of ignited brandy, and bedight with Christmas holly stuck into the top.

Oh, a wonderful pudding! Bob Cratchit said, and calmly too, that he regarded it as the greatest success achieved by Mrs Cratchit since their marriage. Mrs Cratchit said that now the weight was off her mind, she would confess she had had her doubts about the quantity of flour. Everybody had something to say about it, but nobody said or thought it was at all a small pudding for a large family. It would have been flat heresy to do so. Any Cratchit would have blushed at such a thing.

At last the dinner was done, the cloth was cleared, the hearth swept, and the fire made up. The compound in the jug being tasted and considered perfect, apples and oranges were put upon the table, and a shovel-full of chestnuts on the fire. Then all the Cratchit family drew round the hearth, in what Bob Cratchit called a circle, meaning half a one; and at Bob Cratchit's elbow stood the family display of glass; two tumblers, and a custard-cup without a handle. These held the hot stuff from the jug, however, as well as golden goblets would have done; and Bob served it out with beaming looks, while the chestnuts on the fire sputtered and crackled noisily. Then Bob proposed;

'A Merry Christmas to us all, my dears. God bless us!'

Which all the family re-echoed.

'God bless us every one!' said Tiny Tim, the last of all.

He sat very close to his father's side, upon his little stool. Bob held his withered little hand in his, as if he loved the child, and wished to keep him by his side, and dreaded that he might be taken from him.

The Little Match Girl

HANS CHRISTIAN ANDERSEN

It was so dreadfully cold! It was snowing, and the evening was beginning to darken. It was the last evening of the year, too – New Year's Eve. Through the cold and the dark, a poor little girl with bare head and naked feet was wandering along the road. She had, indeed, had a pair of slippers on when she left home; but what was the good of that! They were very big slippers – her mother had worn them last, they were so big – and the little child had lost them hurrying across the road as two carts rattled dangerously past. One slipper could not be found, and a boy ran off with the other – he said he could use it as a cradle when he had children of his own.

So the little girl wandered along with her naked feet red and blue with cold. She was carrying a great pile of matches in an old apron and she held one bundle in her hand as she walked. No one had bought a thing from her the whole day; no one had given her a halfpenny; hungry and frozen, she went her way, looking so woe-begone, poor little thing! The snow-flakes fell upon her long hair that curled so prettily about the nape of her neck, but she certainly wasn't thinking of how nice she looked. Lights were shining from all the windows, and there was a lovely smell of roast goose all down the street, for it was indeed New Year's Eve – yes, and that's what she was thinking about.

Over in a corner between two houses, where one jutted a little farther out into the street than the other, she sat down and huddled together; she had drawn her little legs up under her, but she felt more frozen than ever, and she dared not go home, for she had sold no matches and hadn't got a single penny, and her father would beat her. Besides, it was cold at home, too: there was only the roof over them, and the wind whistled in, although the biggest cracks had been stopped up with straw and rags. Her little hands were almost dead with cold. Ah, a little match might do some good! If she only dared pull one out of the bundle, strike it on the wall, and warm her fingers! She drew one out – Whoosh! – How it spluttered! How it burnt! It gave a warm bright flame, just like a little candle, when she held her hand round it. It was a wonderful light: the little girl thought she was sitting in front of a great iron stove with polished brass knobs and fittings; the fire was burning so cheerfully and its warmth was so comforting – oh, what was that! The little girl had just stretched her feet out to warm them, too, when – the fire went out! The stove disappeared – and she was sitting there with the little stump of a burnt-out match in her hand.

Another match was struck; it burnt and flared, and where the light fell upon it, the wall became transparent like gauze; she could see right into the room where the table stood covered with a shining white cloth and set with fine china, and there was a roast goose, stuffed with prunes and apples, steaming deliciously – but what was more gorgeous still, the goose jumped off the dish, waddled across the floor with knife and fork in its back, and went straight over to the poor girl. Then the match went out, and there was nothing to see but the thick cold wall.

She struck yet another. And then she was sitting beneath the loveliest Christmas tree; it was even bigger and more beautifully decorated than the one she had seen this last Christmas through the glass doors of the wealthy grocer's shop. Thousands of candles were burning on its green branches, and gaily coloured pictures, like those that had decorated the shop-windows, were looking down at her. The little girl stretched out both her hands – and then the match went out; the multitude of Christmas-candles rose higher and higher, and now she saw they were the bright stars – one of them fell and made a long streak of fire across the sky.

'Someone's now dying!' said the little girl, for her old granny, who was the only one that had been kind to her, but who was now dead, had said that when a star falls a soul goes up to God.

Once more she struck a match on the wall. It lit up the darkness round about her, and in its radiance stood old granny, so bright and shining, so wonderfully kind.

'Granny!' cried the little girl. 'Oh, take me with you! I know you'll go away when the match goes out – you'll go away just like the warm stove and the lovely roast goose and the wonderful big Christmas-tree!' And she hastily struck all the rest of the matches in the bundle, for she wanted to keep her granny there, and the matches shone with such brilliance that it was brighter than daylight. Granny had never before been so tall and beautiful; she lifted the little girl up on her arm, and they flew away in splendour and joy, high high up towards heaven. And there was no more cold and no more hunger and no more fear – they were with God.

But in the corner by the house, in the cold of the early morning, the little girl sat, with red cheeks and a smile upon her lips – dead, frozen to death on the last evening of the old year. The morning of the New Year rose over the little dead body sitting there with her matches, one bundle nearly all burnt out. She wanted to keep herself warm, they said; but no one knew what beautiful things she had seen, nor in what radiance she had gone with her old granny into the joy of the New Year.

Christmas Morning

From *Little Women*

LOUISA MAY ALCOTT

Mrs March (Marmee) has four daughters – Meg, Jo, Beth and Amy – whom she calls her 'little women'. Hannah, the family servant, completes this all-female nineteenth-century American household, for father is away at the war. Times are hard, but this is a home that is rich in unselfish love.

Jo was the first to wake in the grey dawn of Christmas morning. No stockings hung at the fireplace, and for a moment she felt as much disappointed as she did long ago, when her little sock fell down because it was so crammed with goodies. Then she remembered her mother's promise and, slipping her hand under her pillow, drew out a little crimson-covered book. She knew it very well, for it was that beautiful old story of the best life ever lived, and Jo felt that it was a true guidebook for any pilgrim going the long journey. She woke Meg with a 'Merry Christmas' and bade her see what was under her pillow. A green-covered book appeared with the same picture inside and a few words written by their mother, which made their one present very precious in their eyes. Presently Beth and Amy woke to rummage and find their little books also – one dove-coloured, the other blue; and all sat looking at and talking about them while the east grew rosy with the coming day.

In spite of her small vanities, Margaret had a sweet and pious nature, which unconsciously influenced her sisters, especially Jo, who loved her very tenderly and obeyed her because her advice was so gently given.

'Girls,' said Meg seriously, looking from the tumbled head beside her to the two little night-capped ones in the room beyond, 'mother wants us to read and love and mind these books, and we must begin at once. We used to be faithful about it, but since father went away and all this war trouble unsettled us, we have neglected many things. You can do as you please, but *I* shall keep my book on the table here and read a little every morning as soon as I wake, for I know it will do me good and help me through the day.'

Then she opened her new book and began to read. Jo put her arm round her and, leaning cheek to cheek, read also, with the quiet expression so seldom seen on her restless face.

'How good Meg is! Come, Amy, let's do as they do. I'll help you with the hard words, and they'll explain things if we don't understand,' whispered Beth, very much impressed by the pretty books and her sisters' example.

'I'm glad mine is blue,' said Amy, and then the rooms were very still while the pages softly turned, and the winter sunshine crept in to touch the bright heads and serious faces with a Christmas greeting.

'Where is mother?' asked Meg, as she and Jo ran down to thank her for their gifts half an hour later.

'Goodness only knows. Some poor creeter come a-beggin', and your ma went straight off to see what was needed. There never *was* such a woman for givin' away vittles and drink, clothes and firin',' replied Hannah, who had lived with the family since Meg was born and was considered by them all more as a friend than a servant.

'She will be back soon, I think, so fry your cakes, and have everything ready,' said Meg, looking over the presents, which were collected in a basket and kept under the sofa, ready to be produced at the proper time. 'Why, where is Amy's bottle of cologne?' she added, as the little flask did not appear.

'She took it out a minute ago and went off with it to put a ribbon on it, or some such notion,' replied Jo, dancing about the room to take the first stiffness off the new army-slippers.

'How nice my handkerchiefs look, don't they? Hannah washed and ironed them for me, and I marked them all myself,' said Beth, looking proudly at the somewhat uneven letters which had cost her such labor.

'Bless the child! she's gone and put "Mother" on them instead of "M. March". How funny!' cried Jo, taking up one.

'Isn't it right? I thought it was better to do it so, because Meg's initials are "M.M.", and I don't want any one to use these but Marmee,' said Beth, looking troubled.

'It's all right, dear, and a very pretty idea – quite sensible, too, for no one can ever mistake now. It will please her very much, I know,' said Meg, with a frown for Jo and a smile for Beth.

'There's mother. Hide the basket, quick!' cried Jo, as a door slammed and steps sounded in the hall.

Amy came in hastily and looked rather abashed when she saw her sisters all waiting for her.

'Where have you been, and what are you hiding behind you?' asked Meg, surprised to see, by her hood and cloak, that lazy Amy had been out so early.

'Don't laugh at me, Jo! I didn't mean anyone should know till the time came. I only meant to change the little bottle for a big one, and I gave *all* my money to get it, and I'm truly trying not to be selfish any more.'

As she spoke, Amy showed the handsome flask which replaced the cheap one and looked so earnest and humble in her little effort to forget herself that Meg hugged her on the spot and Jo pronounced her 'a trump', while Beth ran to the window and picked her finest rose to ornament the stately bottle.

'You see, I felt ashamed of my present, after reading and talking about being good this morning, so I ran round the corner and changed it the minute I was up, and I'm *so* glad, for mine is the handsomest now.'

Another bang of the street door sent the basket under the sofa and the girls to the table, eager for breakfast.

'Merry Christmas, Marmee! Many of them! Thank you for our books; we read some and mean to every day,' they cried, in chorus.

'Merry Christmas, little daughters! I'm glad you began at once

81

and hope you will keep on. But I want to say one word before we sit down. Not far away from here lies a poor woman with a little newborn baby. Six children are huddled into one bed to keep from freezing, for they have no fire. There is nothing to eat over there, and the oldest boy came to tell me they were suffering hunger and cold. My girls, will you give them your breakfast as a Christmas present?'

They were all unusually hungry, having waited nearly an hour, and for a minute no one spoke; only a minute, for Jo exclaimed impetuously –

'I'm so glad you came before we began!'

'May I go and help carry the things to the poor little children?' asked Beth eagerly.

'*I* shall take the cream and the muffins,' added Amy, heroically giving up the articles she most liked.

Meg was already covering the buckwheats and piling the bread into one big plate.

'I thought you'd do it,' said Mrs March, smiling as if satisfied. 'You shall all go and help me, and when we come back we will have bread and milk for breakfast and make it up at dinnertime.'

They were soon ready, and the procession set out. Fortunately it was early, and they went through back streets, so few people saw them, and no one laughed at the queer party.

A poor, bare, miserable room it was, with broken windows, no fire, ragged bedclothes, a sick mother, wailing baby, and a group of pale, hungry children cuddled under one old quilt, trying to keep warm.

How the big eyes stared and the blue lips smiled as the girls went in!

'Ach, mein Gott! It is good angels come to us!' said the poor woman, crying for joy.

'Funny angels in hoods and mittens,' said Jo, and set them laughing.

In a few minutes it really did seem as if kind spirits had been at work there. Hannah, who had carried wood, made a fire and stopped up the broken panes with old hats and her own cloak. Mrs March gave the mother tea and gruel and comforted her with promises of help, while she dressed the little baby as tenderly as if it had been her own. The girls, meantime, spread the table, set the children round the fire, and fed them like so many hungry birds –

laughing, talking, and trying to understand the funny broken English.

'Das ist gut!' 'Die Engel-kinder!' cried the poor things as they ate and warmed their purple hands at the comfortable blaze.

The girls had never been called angel children before and thought it very agreeable, especially Jo, who had been considered a 'Sancho' ever since she was born. That was a very happy breakfast, though they didn't get any of it, and when they went away, leaving comfort behind, I think there were not in all the city four merrier people than the hungry little girls who gave away their breakfasts and contented themselves with bread and milk on Christmas morning.

'That's loving our neighbour better than ourselves, and I like it,' said Meg, as they set out their presents, while their mother was upstairs collecting clothes for the poor Hummels.

Not a very splendid show, but there was a great deal of love done up in the few little bundles, and the tall vase of red roses, white chrysanthemums, and trailing vines, which stood in the middle, gave quite an elegant air to the table.

'She's coming! Strike up, Beth! Open the door, Amy! Three cheers for Marmee!' cried Jo, prancing about, while Meg went to conduct mother to the seat of honor.

Beth played her gayest march, Amy threw open the door, and Meg enacted escort with great dignity. Mrs March was both surprised and touched and smiled with her eyes full as she examined her presents and read the little notes which accompanied them. The slippers went on at once, a new handkerchief was slipped into her pocket, well scented with Amy's cologne, the rose was fastened in her bosom, and the nice gloves were pronounced a 'perfect fit'.

There was a good deal of laughing and kissing and explaining in the simple, loving fashion which makes these home festivals so pleasant at the time, so sweet to remember long afterward...

Christmas Comes to Narnia

From *The Lion, the Witch and the Wardrobe*

C.S. LEWIS

The wicked White Witch has all Narnia in thrall – so it is always winter, but never Christmas! But when Lucy and Edmund, Peter and Susan find their way into Narnia through the back of the wardrobe, things begin to change. Edmund is lured away – but the others team up with Mr and Mrs Beaver and the friends of Aslan, the lion. For Aslan has returned. From their secret hide-out underground, the children hear the sound of jingling bells. Mr Beaver investigates...

'Come on!' cried Mr Beaver, who was almost dancing with delight. 'Come and see! This is a nasty knock for the Witch! It looks as if her power was already crumbling.'

'What *do* you mean, Mr Beaver?' panted Peter as they all scrambled up the steep bank of the valley together.

'Didn't I tell you,' answered Mr Beaver, 'that she'd made it always winter and never Christmas? Didn't I tell you? Well, just come and see!'

And then they were all at the top and did see.

It *was* a sledge, and it *was* reindeer with bells on their harness. But they were far bigger than the Witch's reindeer, and they were not white but brown. And on the sledge sat a person whom everyone knew the moment they set eyes on him. He was a huge man in a bright red robe (bright as holly-berries) with a hood that had fur inside it and a great white beard that fell like a foamy waterfall over his chest. Everyone knew him because, though you see people of his sort only in Narnia, you see pictures of them and hear them talked about even in our world – the world on this side of the wardrobe door. But when you really see them in Narnia it is rather different. Some of the pictures of Father Christmas in our world make him look only funny and jolly. But now that the children actually stood looking at him they didn't find it quite like that. He was so big, and so glad, and so real, that they all became quite still. They felt very glad, but also solemn.

'I've come at last,' said he. 'She has kept me out for a long time, but I have got in at last. Aslan is on the move. The Witch's magic is weakening.'

And Lucy felt running through her that deep shiver of gladness which you only get if you are being solemn and still.

'And now,' said Father Christmas, 'for your presents. There is a new and better sewing-machine for you, Mrs Beaver. I will drop it in your house as I pass.'

'If you please, sir,' said Mrs Beaver, making a curtsey. 'It's locked up.'

'Locks and bolts make no difference to me,' said Father Christmas. 'And as for you, Mr Beaver, when you get home you will find your dam finished and mended and all the leaks stopped and a new sluice-gate fitted.'

Mr Beaver was so pleased that he opened his mouth very wide and then found he couldn't say anything at all.

'Peter, Adam's Son,' said Father Christmas.

'Here, sir,' said Peter.

'These are your presents,' was the answer, 'and they are tools not toys. The time to use them is perhaps near at hand. Bear them well.' With these words he handed to Peter a shield and a sword. The shield was the colour of silver and across it there romped a red lion, as bright as a ripe strawberry at the moment when you pick it. The hilt of the sword was of gold and it had a sheath and a sword belt and everything it needed, and it was just the right size and weight for Peter to use. Peter was silent and solemn as he received these gifts for he felt they were a very serious kind of present.

'Susan, Eve's Daughter,' said Father Christmas. 'These are for you,' and he handed her a bow and quiver full of arrows and a little ivory horn. 'You must use the bow only in great need,' he said, 'for I do not mean you to fight in the battle. It does not easily miss. And when you put this horn to your lips and blow it, then, wherever you are, I think help of some kind will come to you.'

Last of all he said, 'Lucy, Eve's Daughter,' and Lucy came forward. He gave her a little bottle of what looked like glass (but people said afterwards that it was made of diamond) and a small dagger. 'In this bottle,' he said, 'there is a cordial made of the juice of one of the fire-flowers that grow in the mountains of the sun. If you or any of your friends is hurt, a few drops of this will restore them. And the dagger is to defend yourself at great need. For you also are not to be in the battle.'

'Why, sir?' said Lucy. 'I think – I don't know – but I think I could be brave enough.'

'That is not the point,' he said. 'But battles are ugly when women fight. And now' – here he suddenly looked less grave – 'here is something for the moment for you all!' and he brought out (I suppose from the big bag at his back, but nobody quite saw him do it) a large tray containing five cups and saucers, a bowl of lump sugar, a jug of cream, and a great big teapot all sizzling and piping hot. Then he cried out 'Merry Christmas! Long live the true King!' and cracked his whip, and he and the reindeer and the sledge and all were out of sight before anyone realized that they had started.

5

Legends, Folk Tales and Customs

There are all kinds of legends and folk tales about the events
surrounding the Christmas story and what they mean. For
whenever people hear the story new tales are told.
This section brings together stories from central
Europe, from Russia and from the Native Americans.
I have also included some which help to explain where our
Christmas customs come from.

Winds Through the Olive Trees

A traditional French carol

Winds through the olive trees
softly did blow,
round little Bethlehem
long, long ago.

Sheep on the hillsides lay,
white as the snow;
shepherds were watching them
long, long ago.

Then from the happy skies
angels bent low
singging their songs of joy
long, long ago:

For, in his manger bed
cradled, we know,
Christ came to Bethlehem
long, long ago.

A Child is Born

Adapted from an old Christmas legend

JINDRA CAPEK, TRANSLATED BY NOEL SIMON

One cold, clear night, many years ago, when the earth lay frozen under a sky brilliant with stars, three strangely dressed figures could be seen struggling through deep snow.

Hoping to find shelter for the night, the men knocked on the door of a small cottage. It was opened by a shepherd boy, Josh, who cheerfully invited them in.

As they ate their simple meal, and warmed themselves in front of the fire, Josh's visitors told him their story.

'We are three learned men – astronomers – come from afar. We are following a star that has proclaimed the birth of a child who is destined to change the world through love. War and hunger, injustice and fear, will be banished from the earth. There is no mistaking the star's meaning. Guided by it, we are journeying to salute the new king, long and difficult though the route may be.'

Early next morning the three continued on their way, following the star.

Although Josh remained behind, he was deeply impressed by all that he had heard. A child would change the world! Could love really rule men's hearts? His head reeled with questions.

In no time he had made up his mind to follow the three strangers, 'I, too, must greet this child,' he decided. 'The star will show me the way.'

Accompanied by his little cat, Josh hurried to the village. He told of his meeting with the three Wise Men. As he spread the glad tidings, his joy made all the villagers happy, too.

Forgetting their troubles, they started to sing and dance.

'Here, take this flute with you,' one of the villagers said to Josh as he set off. 'Playing it, you will gladden the hearts of all whom you meet, as well as the child's. Tell him about us, and of the faith we have in him.'

The shepherd boy's route took him past a house far from anywhere. Outside, an old man was chopping wood, tired and out of breath. Josh offered to help him, and before long had cut enough wood to last the old man well into the spring.

Josh told the old man the reason for his journey, and about his hopes of finding the miraculous child.

'The winter is cold, and the road very long,' the man said. 'Take this woollen blanket with you to warm yourself and the child, and tell him about me.'

So Josh continued his journey with his little cat, always following the star.

Eventually he met a small girl who was weeping. She had lost her way. Josh comforted her by playing his flute, and helped her to find her parents' house.

The girl's mother flung her arms around her daughter, clasping her tight. Once more Josh told the story of the three Wise Men, and the newborn child that would be the Saviour of the world.

The woman gave him a loaf of freshly baked bread. 'Take this bread and give it to the child,' she said. 'Tell him that we eagerly await his coming,' and she wished Josh a safe journey.

Ever brighter shone the star, and at last Josh realized that he and his cat had come to the end of their journey.

Not everyone had believed his story; some had laughed at him scornfully. Perhaps the Wise Men had been wrong about a new king being born. If so, what would he say on the way home to the disappointed people he had met?

Then, in the distance, he caught sight of a dilapidated stable. The star, to his surprise, appeared to hover directly above it. Seeing the unearthly light shining forth, Josh's heart was filled with happiness.

As he looked through the stable door, Josh recognized the three Wise Men. They were gazing in adoration at a child held in his mother's arms. Tiptoeing forward, Josh gently wrapped the woollen blanket around both the mother and her baby to protect them from the cold. Then he took the loaf of bread and shared it with all who were there.

After bidding everyone farewell, Josh, followed by his cat, set off on the return journey. Walking along, he played so expressive a tune on his flute that those who heard it understood his message. It told of people's troubles, but it also told of great joy, and hope to come, for all mankind.

Baboushka

A traditional Russian folk tale

ARTHUR SCHOLEY

All the villagers were out, bubbling with excitement.

'Did you see it again last night?'

'Of course we did.'

'Much bigger.'

'It was moving, coming towards us. Tonight it will be high above us.'

That night, excitement, like a wind, scurried through the lanes and alleys.

'There's been a message.'

'An army is on the way.'

'Not an army – a procession.'

'Horses and camels and treasure.'

Now everyone was itching for news. No one could work. No one could stay indoors.

No one that is, but Baboushka. Baboushka had work to do – she always had. She swept, polished, scoured and shined. Her house was the best kept, best polished, best washed\ and painted. Her garden was beautiful, her cooking superb.

'All this fuss for a star!' she muttered. 'I haven't time even to look. I'm so behind, I must work all night!'

So, she missed the star at its most dazzling, high overhead. She missed the line of twinkling lights coming towards the village at dawn. She missed the sound of pipes and drums, the tinkling of bells getting louder. She missed the voices and whispers and then the sudden quiet of the villagers, and the footsteps coming up the path to her door. But the knocking! She couldn't miss that.

'Now what?' she demanded, opening the door.

Baboushka gaped in astonishment. There were three kings at her door! And a servant.

'My masters seek a place to rest,' he said. 'Yours is the best house in the village.'

91

'You... want to stay here?'

'It would only be till night falls and the star appears again.'

Baboushka gulped. 'Come in, then,' she said.

How the kings' eyes sparkled at the sight of the home-baked bread, the meat pies, the cakes, jams and pickles.

As she dashed about, serving them, Baboushka asked question after question.

'Have you come a long way?'

'Very far,' sighed Caspar.

'And where are you going?'

'We're following the star,' said Melchior.

'But where?'

They didn't know, they told her. But they believed that it would lead them, in the end, to a new-born king, a king such as the world had never seen before, a king of Earth and Heaven.

'Why don't you come with us?' said Balthasar. 'Bring him a gift as we do. See, I bring gold, and my colleagues bring spices and ointments.'

'Oh,' said Baboushka. 'I am not sure that he would welcome me. And as for a gift...'

'This excellent pickle's fit for any king!' cried Balthasar.

Baboushka laughed. 'Pickle? For a baby? A baby needs toys.' She paused. 'I have a cupboard full of toys,' she said sadly. 'My baby son, my little king, died while very small.'

Balthasar stopped her as she bustled once more to the kitchen.

'This new king could be your king, too. Come with us when the star appears tonight,' he said.

'I'll... I'll think about it,' sighed Baboushka.

As the kings slept, Baboushka cleaned and tidied as quietly as she could. What a lot of extra work there was! And this new king. What a funny idea – to go off with the kings to find him. Yet, could she possibly do it? Leave home and go looking for him just like that?

Baboushka shook herself. No time for dreaming! All this washing-up, and putting away of dishes, and extra cooking. Anyway, how long would she be away? What would she wear? And what about gifts?

She sighed. 'There is so much to do. The house will have to be cleaned when they've gone. I couldn't just leave it.'

Suddenly it was night-time again. There was the star!

'Are you ready, Baboushka?'

'I'll… I'll come tomorrow,' Baboushka called. 'I'll catch up. I must just tidy here, find a gift, get ready…'

The kings waved sadly. The star shone ahead. Baboushka ran back into the house, eager to get on with her work.

Sweeping, dusting, beating all the cushions and carpets, cleaning out the kitchen, cooking – away went the night.

At last she went to the small cupboard, opened the door and gazed sadly once again at all those toys. But, goodness me, how dusty they were! One thing was certain. They weren't fit for a baby king! They would all need to be cleaned. Better get started at once.

On, on, she worked. One by one the toys glowed, glistened and gleamed. There! Now they would be fit for the royal baby.

Baboushka looked through the window. It was dawn! Clear on the air came the sound of the farm cockerel. She looked up. The star had gone. The kings would have found somewhere else to rest by now. She would easily catch them up.

At the moment, though, she felt so tired. Surely she could rest now – just for an hour.

Suddenly she was wide awake. It was dark. She had slept all day! She ran out into the street. No star. She rushed back into the house, pulled on her cloak, hurriedly packed the toys in a basket and stumbled down the path the kings had taken.

On she went, hurrying through village after village. Everywhere she asked after the kings.

'Oh yes,' they told her, 'we saw them. They went that way.'

Days passed and Baboushka lost count. The villages grew bigger and became towns. But Baboushka never stopped, through night and day. Then she came to a city.

The palace! she thought. That's where the royal baby would be born.

'No royal baby here,' said the palace guard.

'Three kings? What about them?' asked Baboushka.

'Ah yes, they came. But they didn't stay long. They were soon on their journey.'

'But where to?'

'Bethlehem, that was the place. I can't imagine why. It's a very poor place. But that's where they went.'

She set off at once.

93

It was evening when Baboushka wearily arrived at Bethlehem. How many days had she been on the journey? She could not remember. And could this really be the place for a royal baby? It didn't look like it. It was not much bigger than her own village. She went to the inn.

'Oh yes,' said the landlord, 'the kings were here, two days ago. There was great excitement. But they didn't even stay the night.'

'And a baby?' Baboushka cried. 'Was there a baby?'

'Yes,' said the landlord, 'there was. Those kings asked to see the baby, too.'

When he saw the disappointment in Baboushka's eyes, he stopped.

'If you'd like to see where the baby was,' he said quickly, 'it was across the yard there. I couldn't offer the poor couple anything better at the time. My inn was packed full. They had to go in the stable.'

Baboushka followed him across the yard.

'Here's the stable,' he said. Then he left her.

'Baboushka?'

Someone was standing in the half-light of the doorway. He looked kindly at her. Perhaps he knew where the family had gone? She knew now that the baby king was the most important thing in the world to her.

'They have gone to Egypt, and safety,' he told Baboushka. 'And the kings have returned to their kingdoms another way. But one of them told me about you. I am sorry but, as you see, you are too late. Shepherds came as soon as the angels told them. The kings came as soon as they saw the star. It was Jesus the Christ-child they found, the world's Saviour.'

It is said that Baboushka is still looking for the Christ-child, for time means nothing in the search for things that are real. Year after year she goes from house to house calling, 'Is he here? Is the Christ-child here?'

Particularly at Christmas, when she sees a sleeping child and hears of good deeds, she will lift out a toy from her basket and leave it, just in case.

Then, on Baboushka goes with her journey, still searching, still calling, 'Is he here? Is the Christ-child here?'

A Christmas Song

PHILLIPS BROOKS

Everywhere, everywhere, Christmas tonight!
Christmas in lands of fir tree and pine;
Christmas in lands of palm tree and vine;
Christmas where snow peaks stand solemn and white;
Christmas where cornfields lie sunny and bright:
Everywhere, everywhere, Christmas tonight!

The Deer on Christmas Eve

Based on a Native American tale

One Christmas Eve in Canada, three Native American children were going through the pinewoods to take a carved wooden pipe to their grandfather as his present for Christmas. There was a little girl aged six, and her older brother and sister who were nine and ten.

It was growing dusk and the moon was just showing above the forest trees. As they went softly along the path one behind the other, they sang a carol. These were the words they were singing:

> *Within a lodge of broken bark*
> *The tender Babe was found,*
> *A ragged robe of rabbit skin*
> *Enwrapped his beauty round;*
> *And as the hunter braves drew nigh,*
> *The angels' song rang loud and high.*

Suddenly the little girl stopped singing. 'Look,' she whispered. The others stopped and looked. In a clearing in the forest, they could see a troop of spotted deer. They seemed to be kneeling down with their heads bowed near the ground.

'Are they praying because it's Christmas Eve?' she asked.

'Of course not, silly,' said her brother. 'They often kneel down like that to eat the grass.'

'I've never seen them,' said the older sister.

The children walked on, singing another verse of their carol:

> *The earliest moon of winter-time*
> *Is not so round and fair*
> *As was the ring of glory*
> *On the tiny Infant there.*
> *The chiefs from far before him knelt,*
> *With gifts of fox and beaver-pelt.*

They were going along a green path now, by the edge of a lake. The little girl stopped again. 'There are some more,' she said. And there were some more young deer. They seemed to be kneeling by the side of the lake, with their heads bowed over the water. 'They *are* saying their prayers,' she said.

'They might be,' said her sister.

'Sillies,' said their brother. 'They're drinking from the lake. I've often seen them do it.'

Just on the other side of the lake stood their grandfather's wigwam. He was glad to see them; and they sat down to watch while he tried out his new pipe.

'I will tell you the Christmas story,' he said, as he sat there puffing at his pipe. And he told them the story as the Native Americans tell it: about a wonderful baby who was born in a shelter of birch-bark, and how the hunters and the braves, and the great chiefs from afar, came to give him presents of furs and coloured feathers. And then their grandfather added a bit to the story which the children had never heard before.

'They do say,' he said puffing at his pipe, 'that on Christmas Eve, all the gentle animals in the forest – the rabbits, the hares and the deer – kneel down and bow their heads and remember Christ the Lord. People say it,' he added. 'Though I've never seen it.'

'We have,' said the little girl.

'Yes, we have,' said her sister.

'M'm, perhaps that's what it was,' said their brother, and he sat there, looking very thoughtful.

Good King Wenceslas

MARILYN BRUCE

Everyone who sings carols at Christmas knows 'Good King Wenceslas'.
Here is the story it tells.

'Peter, the King wants a flagon of hot wine,' shouted the
Chamberlain.

Peter sighed and got up from the fire. Above him the blackened
roof timbers showed where the smoke curled up and escaped
through the holes in the roof. If he closed one eye he could see a
star shining in the sky far above.

Wearily he fetched the wine and made his way up the narrow
spiral staircase to the King's apartments. It was the day after
Christmas, St Stephen's day, and the festivities had meant a lot of
fetching and carrying for the King's pages. When the King left the
hall after the evening meal Peter had hoped he would not be needed
any more that night. All he really wanted to do was to curl up and
go to sleep.

King Wenceslas was standing by the window. Outside the snow
lay deep and frost hung on the trees, making every branch and
twig twinkle and shine in the moonlight. The mountains stood out
black and forbidding on the far side of the forest.

'Come here,' said the King.

Peter put the wine down and went to the window.

'Who's that old man out there, just beyond the castle moat?'

'Probably old Janislav, Sire,' said Peter. 'He lives with his wife
and grandchildren on the edge of the forest. They say his son was
killed by a bear and the children's mother died of a fever just
before Christmas. They're very poor. He collects wood and sells it
for fuel, but I doubt if he'll find very much tonight. Everything is
buried under the snow.'

The King watched the old man for a moment, then said, 'Go
down to the kitchens. I want a large basket filled with meat,
bread, honey, fruit and wine. I also want a very large bundle of

firewood. We shall visit the old man and give him and his family the best Christmas they've ever had. A little late, I know, but that doesn't matter.'

'Yes, Sire,' said Peter.

'I shall wait for you at the castle gate.'

'You're going to deliver it yourself?' said Peter, astonished.

'Certainly,' said the King, 'and you are coming with me.'

Peter did as he was asked. It was even colder outside than he had expected and he was glad of his thick woollen cloak.

They reached the forest. The snow had been falling for several days and was very deep.

Peter shivered. Despite his warm cloak he was bitterly cold and his teeth chattered as he tried to keep up with the King's long strides.

He stumbled over a branch of a tree that had fallen under the weight of the snow and dropped the bundle of firewood. The straps on the baskets of food slipped and it swayed uncomfortably on his back.

'Sire,' he called. 'Please. I can't go on. The snow is too deep and I'm so cold and tired.'

The King waited while Peter picked up the wood and balanced the basket on his back again.

'Keep behind me,' he said kindly. 'Follow exactly in my footsteps and you will find it much easier. Here, give me the wood.'

'Thank you, Sire,' said Peter, gratefully. He gave the bundle of wood to the King and began to walk close behind him, carefully putting his small feet in the King's much larger footprints. He was right. It was much easier now.

They trudged on. The mountains were much nearer now and in the moonlight Peter could see Janislav's little hut.

The King did not seem at all tired by the long walk. He strode up to the cottage door and knocked on it with his staff. An old woman opened it. She was small and bent and her grey hair was mostly hidden beneath a scarf pulled tightly round her head to keep her ears warm. In the room behind her two small children sat on the floor playing with a wooden doll. The fire was almost out.

The old woman recognized the King at once. 'Oh, Sire,' she whispered, awed, and dropped to her knees in front of him.

'My page tells me your son was killed in the forest,' said the King, helping her to her feet. 'I am so sorry.'

'Yes, Sire,' the old woman replied.

'I am also told you are looking after your grandchildren as their mother is also dead.'

The old woman nodded.

'Then please accept this food and wine with our blessing and a very happy Christmas to you all.'

'Oh, Sire,' said the old woman again. 'May the good Lord bless you for your kindness.'

Peter put the basket on the table and dropped the wood on the floor. He threw some onto the fire and at once it crackled and flared, sending warmth into the little room. He looked round. All of his nine years had been spent in the castle. He had not really thought much about how the poor people lived. He did not like what he saw. A table stood in the middle of the room with a loaf of bread on it and some cheese. Along one wall was a truckle bed covered by a rough woollen blanket. The only light came from the fire and two candles on a ledge.

At that moment Janislav arrived carrying the few sticks he had been able to find in the snow. He gasped when he saw what the King had brought and his eyes filled with tears as he knelt before him and thanked him.

It was much easier walking back to the castle. The King's footprints still showed clearly.

'It was lovely to see their faces when we gave them the basket, wasn't it, Sire?' said Peter. 'I am glad I came. I never really thought before about what it must be like to be so very poor. I'm sorry I grumbled about being cold and tired. Using your footprints helped a lot, though. That was a good idea.'

'Always remember,' said the King, gently, 'to do what you can for those less fortunate than yourself. Jesus taught us that. Tonight you found it helped to walk in my footsteps. Walk in his and you will find your way through life will also be easier.'

The Spider's Web

WILLIAM BARCLAY

When Joseph and Mary and Jesus were on their way to Egypt, the story runs, as the evening came they were weary, and they sought refuge in a cave. It was very cold, so cold that the ground was white with hoar frost.

A little spider saw the little baby Jesus, and he wished so much that he could do something for him to keep him warm in the cold night. He decided to do the only thing he could do, to spin his web across the entrance of the cave, to make, as it were, a curtain there.

Along the path there came a detachment of Herod's soldiers, seeking for children to kill to carry out Herod's bloodthirsty order. When they came to the cave, they were about to burst in to search it, to see if anyone was hiding there, but their captain noticed the spider's web. It was covered with the white hoar frost and stretched right across the entrance to the cave.

'Look,' he said, 'at the spider's web there. It is quite unbroken and there cannot possibly be anyone in the cave, for anyone entering the cave would certainly have torn the web.'

So the soldiers passed on, and left the holy family in peace because a little spider had spun his web across the entrance to the cave.

And that, so they say, is why to this day we put tinsel on our Christmas trees, for the glittering tinsel streamers stand for the spider's web, white with the hoar frost, stretched across the cave on the way to Egypt.

A Bright Star Shone

JANIS PRIESTLEY

A
star
shines.
I
am a
fir tree.
Each year at
Christmas, dads come
and buy me.
Children hang bright
baubles, for ev'ryone to see.
Beneath my branches,
piled untidily, gifts in bright
wrappers,
wait for days to be
opened. On that day, a little baby
was born, in a stable, to gentle Mary. There
in Bethlehem, King David's
city. A manger bed was all there seemed to be,
oxen and asses, standing so quietly, worshipped God's dear son
with Joseph's grey donkey.
For
this
baby
king
angels sang sweetly, and a bright
star shone. So sing carols softly,
ev'ry Christmastide.

St Boniface and the Christmas Tree

MARILYN BRUCE

Hans drew his cloak closer round his shoulders and stamped his feet. He was bitterly cold. The frost hung on the trees and it was snowing again.

Tomorrow would be the winter solstice. The night when the old year died. The night when Thor needed a special sacrifice if he was to give back warmth to the earth. Margarethe, Hans' sister of eight summers, had been chosen to be that sacrifice.

Tomorrow night she would be dressed in white with a garland of ivy leaves on her long fair hair. She would be laid on the altar beneath Thor's oak and as the moon rose through its branches, the Chief Druid would plunge the silver dagger into her heart and she would die so that the sun would return to the earth and the crops grow again.

Hans had seen it happen many times before and always hated every minute of it but this year it was different. This year the Druids had chosen Margarethe. He had to do something. He had to save her. But how?

He remembered hearing about a man called Boniface who had come to the forest from England and told of a new god called Jesus who loved everyone and did not want sacrifices. If he could find Boniface maybe this new god could save Margarethe.

He crept away from the circle of huts towards the edge of the village, Gunter, his wolf-hound, at his side. A twig cracked beneath his feet. He froze in the shadows, holding his breath. Something rustled through the dead leaves and a wolf howled somewhere in the forest, but there were no human sounds. He dare not be seen leaving. They would want to know why and if the priests found out... he shuddered at the thought.

He reached the trees and melted into the blackness of the forest. Which way now? Where was Boniface? He had so few hours in which to find him.

The path forked in front of him.

'Which way?' he thought desperately. He picked up a twig and tossed it into the air. It came down in the right hand fork. 'So be it,' said Hans and set off down the new path, Gunter trotting at his heels.

They travelled all night through the forest and just as dawn was breaking he saw the flickering light of a fire ahead. Cautiously he crept towards it, his hand gripping the fur round Gunter's neck. He could feel the dog growling softly. From the shadows he saw a man sitting beside it, cooking a piece of meat. The smell made him feel hungry.

But Hans was afraid. His mouth went dry and little shivers of fear ran up and down his spine. The forest was full of thieves and murderers – everyone said so.

Then Gunter surprised him by trotting forward into the fire-light.

'Hello, boy,' said the man softly. 'Are you hungry too?' He held out his hand. Gunter stopped, then licked the man's outstretched fingers.

Hans came slowly into the open, his heart still thudding in his chest.

'Well, lad,' said the man, 'where have you come from?'

'The forest,' said Hans.

'Are you hungry? Come and share my breakfast. It's not much but you're welcome to it.'

Hans squatted down by the fire, holding out his hands to the warmth.

'You're very young to be out at this hour.'

'I'm ten,' said Hans, his chin sticking out defiantly, 'and I'm nearly a man.'

'Well now, young man of ten, where are you going?'

'I'm looking for Boniface,' he said. 'Have you seen him?'

'Certainly.'

'Where?' shouted Hans, jumping up. 'Where is he? I must find him?'

'Why?'

'You wouldn't understand,' said Hans.

'I might.'

Hans thought for a moment. Should he tell this man? He had a kind face and he had offered to share his breakfast with him. Gunter trusted him. The dog was lying down beside the fire, happily gnawing on a bone the man had thrown to him.

There was something about him Hans could not quite understand. He was so peaceful, so gentle, and yet carried an air of authority. He made up his mind.

'They're going to sacrifice my sister tonight and I must find Boniface to save her.'

'Why do you think Boniface can help?'

'He says God loves everyone and sent the Lord Jesus to save us. If that's true, perhaps he can save my sister, too.'

'Indeed he can, if it is his will.'

'Tell me where Boniface is,' implored Hans.

'He's here.'

'Here? Are you Boniface?'

'Yes,' said the man.

'Oh, sir,' begged Hans, 'come to my village and save my sister. She's only eight and she's to be sacrificed to Thor at the full moon tonight.'

'Where is your village?'

'Back there,' and he pointed back into the forest. 'Is Jesus real?' he asked.

'He's real,' said Boniface, 'but we must hurry if we are to save your sister.'

All day they travelled back through the forest. It was already dark by the time they reached Hans' village.

Torches had been lit and the people were gathered in front of the altar before the mighty oak. Any minute now the moon would rise.

A hut door opened and Margarethe was led out by the priest and slowly they moved towards the altar on which already lay the silver dagger. Hans made to rush forward but Boniface put his hand on his shoulder.

'Trust God,' he smiled.

As the procession reached the altar two priests lifted Margarethe onto it. She screamed, terrified.

Boniface took a little wooden cross from his girdle and holding it in front of him strode across the clearing.

'No,' he thundered, 'the Lord said, you must not kill. He also said you must not worship false gods. Thor is a false god.'

The crowd murmured angrily.

Boniface looked around. A huge axe lay on the ground. He

picked it up and swung it hard against the oak. Its head buried itself in the enormous trunk. Again and again he struck.

The crowd gasped.

The great tree creaked and groaned and began to sway, and with a thunderous crash it fell to the ground. The priests backed away in fear.

Then there was silence.

Nothing and no one moved.

The people could not understand it. What was happening? This man had cut down Thor's oak. He had cheated Thor of his sacrifice but the god had done nothing about it. He should at least have sent a thunderbolt to strike the man dead!

Margarethe still lay trembling on the altar. Very gently Boniface helped her down onto the ground. As he did so he noticed a tiny fir tree growing among the roots of the fallen tree, its green needles glistening in the light of the torches.

He turned to face the people. 'Listen to me. The Lord Jesus came to earth as a little child to point the way to heaven. Look, this tiny tree is doing the same thing. The fir tree is a tree of peace. It gives shelter to the birds in winter, you use its wood to make your homes and its cones to light and scent your fires. Make this tree your special tree. Tomorrow is Christmas Day. Do you know what that means?'

The crowd were silent, watching him. He told them about Christmas and the Baby born in the stable. He told of the shepherds and the Wise Men and the people listened in wonder.

Overhead the stars twinkled and shone.

Next day the little village celebrated Christmas and they called the fir tree the Christmas tree.

The Christmas Tree

An Australian carol

JOHN WHEELER

Christmas Day where e'er you be,
Light your candles on the Tree
Set it up for all to see,
To the Lord of Light above;
Like the birds in happy flight
Children dance in golden light,
Deck the Tree for their delight,
On this Day of Heav'nly Love.
Christmas Day, where e'er you be,
Light your candles on the Tree.

When the summer night is here,
Like a lantern burning clear
Ev'ry window, far and near,
Shining forth its Tree of Love;
Glory to the Heav'nly Name,
Glory to the Star that came
Over Beth'lem like a flame –
Glory to the Light above!
Christmas Day, where e'er you be,
Light your candles on the Tree.

A Mouse and a Song

JEAN WATSON

The children in the little Austrian village of Oberndorf were far too excited to be good and quiet. They were spinning like tops. They were as high as kites. Because today was Christmas Eve and tomorrow would be Christmas Day. For weeks the air had been humming with secrets and now gaily-wrapped packages lay piled around the Christmas trees.

Inside the houses, there were glowing fires and happy people. Outside, it was cold and snowy and there was very little food for the creatures who lived in the fields and woods. One of these was a very hungry field-mouse. His search for nuts and berries brought him to the village church. In its huge wooden door was a crack, just big enough for a very hungry field-mouse to squeeze through.

But inside the building, it was dark and strange. The mouse pattered here and there but could find nothing to fill his empty stomach. He came across some big, metal pipes.

'No food here,' he thought. But then he found something soft and began to nibble it. It was chewy but it tasted awful. So after a few mouthfuls he curled up and went to sleep.

But he was too hungry to sleep for long and soon he was pattering down the aisle towards the huge door. The crack was big enough for a very, very hungry field-mouse to squeeze through quite easily. Outside once more, he continued to hunt for food. And of course, he had no idea of where he'd been or what he'd done or what happened afterwards.

The first thing that happened was that Franz, the organist, came into the church. He wanted to practise the carols which the choir would soon be singing there. He sat down at the organ and pressed the big white keys. No sound came out of the organ. He tried again. Still no sound.

'This is terrible!' thought Franz.

Just then Joseph, the minister of the church, came in.

'Hey, Joseph!' called Franz. 'There's something wrong with the organ.'

Joseph hurried up the aisle. Both men went round to the back of the organ. They soon found the hole nibbled by the very hungry field-mouse. It was in the bellows. Usually they pumped air into the organ so that the notes could be heard. But now the air was escaping through the hole, so the bellows couldn't do their job.

'What am I going to do?' asked Franz. 'It's Christmas Eve and people will be coming from all around for the carol service tonight. How can we have any carols without an organ?'

Joseph thought for a moment. Then he said, 'Perhaps we could do something different.'

'What do you mean?' asked Franz.

'Well,' said Joseph. 'Not long ago I visited a home where a mother was holding her new-born baby in her arms. It was a beautiful scene and made me think of the first Christmas. So I went home and wrote a song about it. Perhaps you could write some music for it.'

Franz shrugged, as if to say, 'What would be the point?' But Joseph went on, 'Not organ music. Guitar music. We could give them a new song with a new kind of tune and accompaniment. What do you think, Franz?'

'Guitar music in church!' exclaimed Franz. But he took the paper that Joseph handed to him. As he read the words of the new song, Franz got more and more excited.

'But, Joseph, this is beautiful!' he exclaimed, turning to his friend. 'I can't wait to write the music!'

Soon he was rushing home, through the snow, eager to make up a tune for the new song.

When the people came into the church for the carol service, they were puzzled. Why wasn't the organ playing? Where was Franz, the organist?

They all sat down and waited.

Then, into the church came Franz, with his guitar.

'Tonight we have something very special for you. A new song with new words and music. I will sing it to you first.'

And this is what he sang and played to them:

Silent night, holy night!
All is calm, all is bright,
Round yon virgin, mother and child,
Holy infant so tender and mild,
Sleeping in heavenly peace,
Sleeping in heavenly peace.

Silent night, holy night,
Shepherds quake at the sight,
Glory streams from heaven afar,
Heavenly hosts sing, 'Alleluia,
Christ the Saviour is born,
Christ the Saviour is born.'

Silent night, holy night,
Son of God, Love's pure light,
Radiance beams from thy holy face,
With the dawn of redeeming grace,
Jesus, Lord, at thy birth,
Jesus, Lord, at thy birth.

Everyone, children and grown-ups, loved the new song. The tune and words went together so well that they were soon singing it at the tops of their voices. It was going to be a good carol service, they decided, even without the organ.

A few days later, the organ repair man arrived from another village. He mended the hole in the bellows.

'Would you like to try your organ now?' he asked Franz.

So Franz sat down and played and sang the new song.

'Oh, I like that!' exclaimed the organ repair man. 'I couldn't have a copy of it to take back to my village, could I?'

'You certainly could,' said Franz.

The people in the organ repair man's village, Zillertal, liked the new song as much as the people in Oberndorf did. They all wanted copies of it.

And it didn't stop there. A glove-maker and his family lived in Zillertal but often travelled round to other places. And wherever they went, the new song went. In each place, while the glove-maker sold his gloves, his four musical daughters would sing for the people. And one of the songs that they sang was the one by Franz and Joseph. So more and more people heard it – and loved it.

And now, more than a hundred and fifty years later, people all over the world love 'Silent Night'. It is sung by thousands of people every Christmas. But they don't all know what that lovely song has to do with a very hungry field mouse who, one snowy night, nibbled a hole in the bellows of a church organ.

But you know now, don't you?

The First Christingle

MARILYN BRUCE

Long ago in Czechoslovakia, a very poor family lived on the edge of a village. It was nearly Christmas and there was to be a special service in the church. Each child had been asked to bring a gift to lay beside the manger. Jan and Stefan, Petra and Katya had no gift to take and there was certainly no money to buy one.

Petra sighed. 'What shall we do? If we don't go we shall be in trouble with Father Thomas. But if we do go we won't have a gift to take and all the other children will laugh at us.'

'Could we make something?' suggested Stefan.

'Maybe,' said Jan who was the eldest.

The days passed and the day of the special service arrived but still they had nothing to take.

Little Katya, the youngest of the four, came back from the village.

'Some of the children are taking fruit for the baby,' she said. 'Couldn't we take something like that too?'

'Of course,' said Petra. 'What a good idea. Why ever didn't we think of that. It's so simple.' But it wasn't quite as easy as that.

When they looked round the room all they could find was one orange and that was going bad at the top.

'We can't take that,' said Stefan.

'Yes we can,' said Jan. 'We'll cut out the bad bit. It's only the skin.'

He got a sharp knife and cut round the rotten part of the orange, but it left a hole.

'Let's turn it into a lantern,' suggested Petra. 'If we put a candle in the top no one will know.'

'That's brilliant,' said Stefan and he ran to get a candle from the cupboard.

'It needs something else,' said Petra.

'Here, have my ribbon,' said Katya, and she pulled a bright red ribbon from off her long, dark hair.

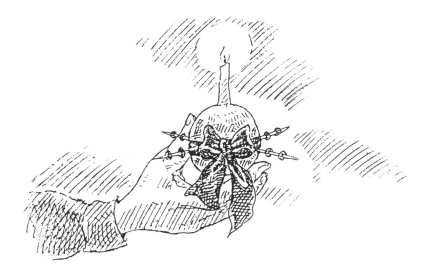

They tied Katya's ribbon round the middle of the orange, but
it kept slipping off. Then Stefan found four little sticks. He sharp-
ened the ends and stuck them into the orange through the ribbon.
They pointed out in all directions, but it still didn't look quite
right.

'There's some raisins in this dish,' said Jan. 'Thread them on
the sticks.' They did so and it looked much better.

'It's a funny looking lantern,' said Petra.

'Never mind,' said Jan, 'it's the best we can do. I think it looks
rather nice. Now we'll have to hurry or we'll be late for the service.'

They quickly tidied themselves up and Petra brushed Katya's
hair until it shone. Without its ribbon it fell in long, thick strands
down her back. Then they went to join the other children from the
village as everyone made their way into the little church where the
manger with its figures of Mary, Joseph and the baby stood before
the altar. Some of the children had expensive toys or rich perfumes
to lay before the infant King, but no one had a lantern quite like
the one Jan was carefully carrying.

'Our lantern doesn't look quite so good now, does it?' whispered
Petra.

'It's fine,' said Stefan, squeezing her hand. 'Don't worry.'

The other children looked at the four curiously. Some even
started to giggle and others pointed rudely and laughed out loud.

'What do you call that?' asked one.

'Is that the best you could do?' asked another.

The children said nothing. They wished they had not come.

At last the time came for everyone to lay their gifts beside the manger. Slowly they moved nearer, little Katya carrying the orange now.

'What is this?' asked Father Thomas as they reached the altar.

'We had no money to buy a gift,' explained Jan, 'so we made the Christ Child a lantern.'

'It's beautiful,' said Father Thomas, as he took it from Katya's hands. He looked at it thoughtfully for a moment and then said, 'But it's much more than just a lantern.'

He turned to the altar and lit the candle in the top of the orange. The flame burned straight and tall. 'Listen,' he said as he turned back to face the congregation, 'these children have brought a wonderful gift. This little lantern tells us so much. Can you see? The orange itself is round like the world and the candle in the top is the light of God shining out all over everyone. These four little sticks point east, west, north and south, reminding us that no one is left out of God's love, and the raisins tell us that he sends the rain and sun to grow our food that makes us strong and well. But the ribbon round the middle is the most important of all – a red ribbon, symbolizing the blood of Jesus that was shed for everyone on that first Good Friday. You children have made a most wonderful gift for the manger, more wonderful than any other brought today. Thank you very much indeed.'

The children were amazed and delighted. Who would have thought that Father Thomas would think that their little lantern was the very best gift of all?

And from that time on, an orange lantern was always placed before the manger in that little town in Czechoslovakia and they called it a Christingle.

6
Christmas Past

'What was Christmas like when you were young?' we ask our mums and dads. Gran's and Grandad's memories are even more fascinating. So this section brings together some stories which tell us about real Christmases, not so very long ago.

A Farmhouse Christmas

From *The Country Child*

ALISON UTTLEY

*Susan Garland is an only child, living in an old farmhouse
deep in the country. To get to school in the nearest village she
must walk for more than a mile across the fields and through
a dark wood. Margaret in this story is Susan's mother, Mrs
Garland. Tom Garland is her father. Joshua, Becky and Dan,
who work in the house and on the farm, all share in this
family Christmas.*

Susan heard the alarm go off in her father's room and Dan's bell
go jingle-jangle. Five o'clock... The wind swished softly against the
window, and thumps and thuds sounded on the stairs...

She was awakened again by the rattle of milk-cans below her
window. Joshua and Becky were coming back with the milk, and it
really was Christmas Day. All else was strangely silent, for the deep
snow deadened the sound of footsteps. She jumped out of bed,
pressed her nose against the window, and rubbed away the Jack
Frost pictures. Everything was blue, and a bright star shone. From
a window in the farm buildings a warm gleam fell on the snow.
Dan was milking the last cow by the light of the lantern which
hung on the wall.

Then she heard his cheerful whistle and the low moo of the
cows as he came out with the can.

What had the cattle done all night? Did they know it was
Christmas? Of course, all God's creatures knew. Becky said the
cows and horses knelt down on Christmas Eve. She could see
them going down on their front knees, the cows so easily, the
horses so painfully, for their legs were wrong.

Sheep knelt when they had foot-rot, it would be easy for them.
But down they all went, bowing to the New Saviour as she bowed
to the new moon.

She washed in the basin with blue daisies round the rim, but she could see neither water nor soap. Candles were for night, not morning use. She brushed her hair in front of the ghost of a mirror, where a white little face looked like a flower-in-the-night. She slipped the round comb through her hair and put on her Sunday honey-combed dress with seven tucks in the skirt and two in the sleeves, a preparation for a long and lanky Susan.

Then she buttoned her slippers and said her short morning prayer, and down she tripped with her stocking-load of presents and the five parcels...

'A merry Christmas, a merry Christmas,' she called, kissing everybody except Dan, which wouldn't be proper. 'Merry' was the word Susan liked, not the limp word, 'happy'.

She presented her paper parcels all round and sat down on the settle to watch the different faces. Dan opened his quickly in the passage and took out a pencil. He licked the point, wrote on the back of his hairy hand, stuck it behind his ear, and grinned his thanks as he went off with his churn.

Becky had a pen-wiper, made out of a wishing-bone and a piece of Margaret's black skirt, and a quill pen cut from a goose feather.

'Just what I wanted,' she cried nobly, for she didn't write a letter once a year, the reason being that she couldn't.

Old Joshua had a tiny bottle of scent, 'White Heather'.

'Thank you kindly, Susan,' said he, as he held up the minute bottle between his big finger and thumb, and struggled with the infinitesimal cork which was too small for him to grip. 'It will come in handy when I clean out the cows.'

To her mother she gave a text, painted by herself, and framed in straw and woolwork.

'O Death, where is thy sting? Where, Grave, thy Victory?'

She had spent many secret hours making this, and she looked anxiously to see what her mother thought of it.

A flicker passed over Mrs Garland's face as she kissed her cheek.

'It's very beautiful, my dear. Why did you choose the text?'

'Because it made me think of summer, of bees and wasps,' replied Susan with a joyful smile.

Her father's present was a big blue handkerchief with his initials embroidered in the corner, T.G.

Then Becky brought from out of the copper tea-urn a string of blue glass beads which she had bought for Susan at Mellow and hidden for months. Mrs Garland gave her a work-box like a house whose roof lifted off and inside there lay little reels of black and white cotton and a tin thimble. And, most startling, the chimney was a red velvet pin-cushion!

But Joshua's present was the most wonderful. It was nothing else than the purse with mother-of-pearl sides and red lining which she had seen at Broomy Vale and coveted so long. A miracle...

The postman came through the wood with a bundle of letters and Christmas cards. He stood by the fire and had a cup of tea, and admired the decorations whilst Margaret opened her letters with cries of happiness, and excitement. She didn't stop to read them, she took out all the cards which had no names on them and popped them into envelopes. Then she readdressed them, dextrously reshuffling and redealing, so that the postman should take them with him, a thrifty procedure.

Susan had a card which she liked above everything, a church with roof and towers and foreground covered in glittering snow. But when it was held up to the light, colours streamed through the windows, reds and blues, from two patches at the back. She put it with her best treasures to be kept for ever.

It was nearly time to start for church and all was bustle and rush as usual. Margaret dressed herself in her plum-coloured merino trimmed with velvet, and dived under the bed for the bonnet-box from which she took her best bonnet and the sealskin muff. It was always wrapped up in a linen handkerchief with a sprig of lavender and lad's love, it was so precious.

Susan dragged on her brown coat running downstairs as she pulled at the sleeves, and her beaver hat with silky pom-poms at the side. She wanted to kiss her father once more under the kissing-bunch before she went.

Then everybody began to run, last-minute directions about the turkey and the stuffing, hunts for threepenny-bits, for Prayer Books, for handkerchiefs and lozenges, Joshua bumping into Susan's hat, Becky letting the milk boil over, Tom shouting, 'You'll be late again, and Christmas morning', and Susan running to play 'Christians awake' in the parlour, at the last minute, but they got off before the bells began to ring.

Down the hill they went, Mrs Garland first, Susan walking in her tracks, through the clean snow, like the page in 'Good King

Wenceslas', along the white roads unmarked except by the hoofs and wheels of the milk carts, to the tune of gay dancing bells to the ivy-covered church...

There was some secret abroad, Susan felt it as soon as they got home, by the odd silence, and the knowing glances she intercepted between Joshua and her father. The house tingled with it.

'Susan, go into the parlour and bring out my concertina,' said Tom, when Susan had put her gloves and Prayer Book in the bureau in the hall, and hung up her hat.

'What do you want a concertina now for, Tom?' asked Mrs Garland astonished, but such a flock of winks and nods flew about the room, she followed Susan across the hall.

'Mind it doesn't bite you,' called Tom.

In the middle of the table was a Christmas tree, alive and grow-ing, looking very much surprised at itself, for had not Tom dug it up from the plantation whilst they were at church, and brought it in with real snow on its branches? The rosiest of apples and the nicest yellow oranges were strung to its boughs, and some sugar biscuits with pink icing and a few humbugs from Tom's pocket lay on the snow, with a couple of gaily coloured texts and a sugar elephant. On the top of the tree shone a silver bird, a most aston-ishing silver glass peacock with a tail of fine feathers, which might have flown in at the window, he wouldn't say Nay and he wouldn't say Yea.

Susan was amazed. If an angel from heaven had sat on the table she would have been less surprised. She ran to hug every-body, her heart was full.

They had been so busy getting ready, for Tom only thought of it when Dan was telling him the station gossip of Mrs Drayton's Christmas tree, they had neglected the dinner.

'Dang it,' Tom had said, 'we will have a Christmas tree, too. Go and get the spade, Dan.'

The ground had been like iron, the tree had spreading roots, but they had not harmed the little thing, and it was going back again to the plantation when Christmas was over.

The turkey was not basted, and the bread-sauce was forgotten, but everyone worked with a will and soon all was ready and piping hot.

The potatoes were balls of snow, the sprouts green as if they had just come from the garden, as indeed they had, for they too had been dug out of the snow not long before. The turkey was brown and crisp, it had been Susan's enemy for many a day, chasing her from the poultry-yard, and now it was brought low; the stuffing smelled of summer and the herb garden in the heat of the sun.

As for the plum pudding with its spray of red berries and shiny leaves and its hidden sixpence, which would fall out, and land on Susan's plate, it was the best they had ever tasted...

Outside the world was amazingly blue, light blue snow, indigo trees, deep blue sky, misty blue farm and haystacks, and men with lanterns and bundles of hay on their backs for the horses and cows, or yokes across their shoulders as they went milking...

Susan pressed her nose to the cold window-pane until it became a flat white button, and her breath froze into feathery crystals. 'This is Christmas Day, it's Christmas Day, it won't come again for a whole year. It's Christmas,' she murmured...

Becky washed up and cleared away tea before she got ready for chapel... Then Tom roused himself from his contemplation of the fire and came out to reach down the best lantern and get it ready. It hung between the old pointed horn lantern and Susan's little school lantern, a black shining case with cut-glass sides and a clean fine window at the front. He opened the back and put in a fresh piece of candle from the candle bark, and lit it.

The three set out with muffs, cloaks, walking-sticks, Prayer Books and Bibles, hymn-books, lozenges, clean handkerchiefs folded neatly, the lantern, and three pairs of old woollen stocking legs which they pulled over their boots to keep themselves from slipping. And even then Susan had to run back for the matches.

Becky walked in front with the lantern and a stick, Susan came next, and Mrs Garland last...

The lights streamed from the church windows, straight across the graveyard, and in reds and blues the crucified Christ hung there.

'But He doesn't know about that yet,' thought Susan. 'He's only just born, a Baby a day old. I know more than He knows. I know He will be crucified and He doesn't know yet.'

It was a disturbing thought, which shattered her as she crunched the snow under her feet and stumbled along under the church walls. She wondered if she could warn him, tell him to go back to Heaven, quick, before He was caught by Judas. But of course she couldn't!

The lights dazzled their eyes as they walked up the aisle, Margaret gliding quietly to her place, Susan tiptoeing behind her. Lamps hung from the walls and every dark holly leaf was a candle, every scarlet berry a farthing dip. The windows alone had lost their radiance, and stood back behind the colour and warmth which filled the church, almost visible to the child's eyes searching the air for invisible things, for God on the altar, and angels floating above the choir, for music beating its wings in the high dark beams of the roof, and for goodness and mercy running hand-in-hand down the chancel.

The service was different from the morning service, too. Everybody sang mightily, the deep voices of the old men and the tiny piping voices of children overpowering the organ and compelling it to a slow grandeur in 'While shepherds watched', and 'Hark! the herald angels sing', and 'Lead, kindly light'. They wouldn't be hurried for anyone, and Samuel Robinson must slacken his pace, going on as if he wanted to catch a train!

The old words rang out bravely, and the scent of bear's grease and peppermint balls filled the air like incense...

But the end was coming, they sang a carol, and knelt a few minutes in silence. Margaret poured out her heart to God, asking His help in the thousand anxieties which lay before her, the winter and its dangers, spring and the birds, the harvest, and Susan knelt wrapped in the beauty of the season, thinking of the Christ-Child.

Then the villagers rose to their feet and passed out of church, to greet each other in the porch and find their mufflers, sticks, and pattens. Margaret lighted the lantern and they pulled their stockings over their shoes in the confusion of the crowd. Becky waited for them at the gate, and they called, 'Good night, good night. A happy Christmas and many of them. A happy Christmas and a prosperous New Year when it comes. Same to you and many of them', as they turned away to the darkness.

Christmas at the Little House in the Big Woods

From *Little House in the Big Woods*

LAURA INGALLS WILDER

Laura and her older sister Mary live in the little log cabin Pa has built in the Big Woods of Wisconsin.
'The great, dark trees of the Big Woods stood all around the house... As far as a man could go to the north in a day, or a week, or a whole month, there was nothing but woods.'
There were no houses or roads or people. To east and west there were miles and miles of trees, with only a few scattered log cabins. But Aunt Eliza and Uncle Peter and the cousins were not so very far away.

Aunt Eliza and Uncle Peter and the cousins, Peter and Alice and Ella, were coming to spend Christmas.

The day before Christmas they came. Laura and Mary heard the gay ringing of sleigh bells, growing louder every moment, and then the big bobsled came out of the woods and drove up to the gate. Aunt Eliza and Uncle Peter and the cousins were in it, all covered up, under blankets and robes and buffalo skins.

They were wrapped up in so many coats and mufflers and veils and shawls that they looked like big, shapeless bundles.

When they all came in, the little house was full and running over. Black Susan ran out and hid in the barn, but Jack leaped in circles through the snow, barking as though he would never stop. Now there were cousins to play with!...

They played so hard all day that when night came they were too excited to sleep. But they must sleep, or Santa Claus would not come. So they hung their stockings by the fireplace, and said their prayers, and went to bed – Alice and Ella and Mary and Laura all in one bed on the floor.

Peter had the trundle bed, Aunt Eliza and Uncle Peter were

going to sleep in the big bed, and another bed was made on the attic floor for Pa and Ma. The buffalo robes and all the blankets had been brought in from Uncle Peter's sled, so there were enough covers for everybody...

In the morning they all woke up almost at the same moment. They looked at their stockings, and something was in them. Santa Claus had been there. Alice and Ella and Laura in their red flannel nightgowns and Peter in his red flannel nightshirt, all ran shouting to see what he had brought.

In each stocking there was a pair of bright red mittens and there was a long flat stick of red-and-white-striped peppermint candy, all beautifully notched along each side.

They were all so happy they could hardly speak at first. They just looked with shining eyes at those lovely Christmas presents. But Laura was happiest of all. Laura had a rag doll.

She was a beautiful doll. She had a face of white cloth with black button eyes. A black pencil had made her eyebrows, and her cheeks and her mouth were red with the ink made from pokeberries. Her hair was black yarn that had been knit and ravelled, so that it was curly.

She had little red flannel stockings and little black cloth gaiters for shoes, and her dress was pretty pink and blue calico.

She was so beautiful that Laura could not say a word. She just held her tight and forgot everything else. She did not know that everyone was looking at her, till Aunt Eliza said:

'Did you ever see such big eyes!'

The other girls were not jealous because Laura had mittens, and candy *and* a doll, because Laura was the littlest girl, except Baby Carrie and Aunt Eliza's little baby, Dolly Varden. The babies were too small for dolls. They were so small they did not even know about Santa Claus. They just put their fingers in their mouths and wriggled because of all the excitement.

Laura sat down on the edge of the bed and held her doll. She loved her red mittens and she loved the candy, but she loved her doll best of all. She named her Charlotte.

Then they all looked at each other's mittens, and tried on their own, and Peter bit a large piece out of his stick of candy, but Alice and Ella and Mary and Laura licked theirs, to make it last longer...

Ma said, 'Laura, aren't you going to let the other girls hold your doll?' She meant, 'Little girls must not be so selfish.'

So Laura let Mary take the beautiful doll, and then Alice held her a minute, and then Ella. They smoothed the pretty dress and admired the red flannel stockings and the gaiters, and the curly woollen hair. But Laura was glad when at last Charlotte was safe in her arms again.

Pa and Uncle Peter had each a pair of new, warm mittens, knit in little squares of red and white. Ma and Aunt Eliza had made them.

Aunt Eliza had brought Ma a large red apple stuck full of cloves. How good it smelled! And it would not spoil, for so many cloves would keep it sound and sweet.

Ma gave Aunt Eliza a little needle-book she had made, with bits of silk for covers and soft white flannel leaves into which to stick the needles. The flannel would keep the needles from rusting.

They all admired Ma's beautiful bracket, and Aunt Eliza said that Uncle Peter had made one for her – of course, with different carving.

Santa Claus had not given them anything at all. Santa Claus did not give grown people presents, but that was not because they had not been good. Pa and Ma were good. It was because they were grown up, and grown people must give each other presents...

Today the weather was so cold that they could not play outdoors, but there were the new mittens to admire, and the candy to lick. And they all sat on the floor together and looked at the pictures in the Bible, and the pictures of all kinds of animals and birds in Pa's big green book. Laura kept Charlotte in her arms the whole time.

Then there was the Christmas dinner. Alice and Ella and Peter and Mary and Laura did not say a word at table, for they knew that children should be seen and not heard. But they did not need to ask for second helpings. Ma and Aunt Eliza kept their plates full and let them eat all the good things they could hold.

'Christmas comes but once a year,' said Aunt Eliza.

Dinner was early, because Aunt Eliza, Uncle Peter, and the cousins had such a long way to go.

'Best the horses can do,' Uncle Peter said, 'we'll hardly make it home before dark.'

So as soon as they had eaten dinner, Uncle Peter and Pa went to put the horses to the sled, while Ma and Aunt Eliza wrapped up the cousins.

They pulled heavy woollen stockings over the woollen stockings and the shoes they were already wearing. They put on mittens and coats and warm hoods and shawls, and wrapped mufflers around their necks and thick woollen veils over their faces. Ma slipped piping hot baked potatoes into their pockets to keep their fingers warm, and Aunt Eliza's flat-irons were hot on the stove, ready to put at their feet in the sled. The blankets and the quilts and the buffalo robes were warmed, too.

So they all got into the big bobsled, cosy and warm, and Pa tucked the last robe well in around them.

'Good-bye! Good-bye!' they called, and off they went, the horses trotting gaily and the sleigh bells ringing.

In just a little while the merry sound of the bells was gone, and Christmas was over. But what a happy Christmas it had been!

A Vicarage Christmas

From *A Vicarage Family*

NOEL STREATFEILD

A Vicarage Family is the story of Noel Streatfeild's own childhood. She is 'Victoria' in this story of the family's first Christmas – and Vicky's birthday – in a new parish. Vicky is the awkward one in the family. She usually feels misunderstood and hard done by, especially by her mother. But she can always count on Annie, the cook.

Victoria's birthday passed, as usual, with one long scurry to get everything done in time.

'It's a shame,' said Annie, who had witnessed the glory of the other birthdays at St Margaret's Bay. 'Proper cheated you've been, with only Irish stew for your dinner and your cake to be the Christmas cake tomorrow. But Annie's not lettin' you down.'

'I know, angel Annie,' said Victoria, looking at the hideous pink vase Annie had given her. 'It's a gorgeous present.'

'I'm not talkin' about the present. It's something else.'

'What?'

'Curiosity killed the cat. You wait and see, and if anyone's sarky about it that's up to them.'

Annie's secret came out at lunch time for, the Irish stew cleared away, Hester with a flourish put a dish of meringues bursting with cream in front of the children's mother.

'What's this?' she asked. Then she turned to Miss Herbert. 'I asked you to tell Annie we'd have baked apples.'

Miss Herbert flushed.

'And so I did. Is it likely I would order rich food like that on Christmas Eve?'

The children's father beamed at Victoria.

'I expect it's Vicky's birthday treat. Even if it is Christmas Eve no doubt you can manage a meringue, can't you, Vicky?'

But the children's mother was still annoyed. Brought up during the rest of the year on plain food her family were all too often, if not ill, cross after Christmas and Victoria, who suffered from what were then called bilious attacks, had been known to be ill for days. Grudgingly she put a meringue on each plate.

'Tell Annie I'll see her after lunch.'

The feeling of disapproval made the meringues slip down less easily than usual and it was hard to find conversation to go with them, so it was quite a relief when the dining-room door was flung open and Annie, very dignified, looking all of her five-foot-two, stalked in.

'You was wanting me, ma'am?'

The last thing the children's mother wanted was to interview Annie in front of the family.

'Yes. I ordered baked apples.'

Up shot Annie's chin.

'So you did. But I like to see justice done. I made meringues for Miss Louise's birthday and chocolate éclairs for Miss Isobel's. What's Miss Vicky done to be palmed off with baked apples?'

The children's mother felt quite intimidated.

'But it's not your place to decide what is eaten. And where did you get the materials?'

'It's everybody's place to see fair's fair. I ordered the meringue cases and the cream same as I did at St Margaret's Bay for Miss Louise's birthday.'

There was really nothing more the children's mother could say unless she gave Annie notice, and she had no intention of doing that. Then the children's father took a hand.

'All right, Annie, you meant well. But next year ask before you choose what pudding we have for Miss Vicky's birthday luncheon.'

Annie, head up, totally unbowed, strutted to the door. There she turned and winked at Victoria.

'Someone has to stick up for you, don't they, ducks? I reckon it's lucky you've got Annie.'

When Annie had gone back to the kitchen and the kitchen door was shut the children's father's face crinkled, then his shoulders began to shake.

'Dear Annie!' he said. 'She is a character. Please, Vicky, try hard not to let her down by being sick on Boxing Day.'

'How could I be?' said Victoria. 'Isn't it the day of the play?'

*   *   *

Another feature of that Christmas was the curate. Curates came and curates went and, except on special occasions, the children seldom saw them to talk to because their father kept his curates' noses to the grindstone. But the curates usually came to Christmas lunch and, unless they had anywhere better to go, stayed on for tea and the Christmas tree – and dull and shy the children found them.

That year the curate – a man called Plimsol, known to the children as Mr Cassock because he seldom seemed to wear anything else – came to lunch. Right away he set a new standard for curates by arriving with five boxes of Fuller's chocolates. A box of chocolates of their own was highly thought of by the children, for most of the boxes received were family boxes and were stored in a cupboard to be passed round before bed, when each child was allowed one. So individual boxes from which the children were allowed, with permission, to help themselves were much valued. But that was not all; when the crackers were pulled Mr Plimsol found a blue sun-bonnet in his and not only put it on but sang: 'Oh, what have you got for dinner, Mrs Bond?' in a delightfully silly way.

'Bags I you for my team for charades this evening,' said cousin John.

Always for Christmas tea and the tree afterwards the vicarage doors were thrown open to those who were lonely or had nowhere else to go. Annie, on hearing the Christmas arrangements, made a remark which became a family quotation: 'As at Sandringham.'

Either because of the success of Mr Plimsol in the charades or because some special quality surrounded that Christmas, it stayed in the children's memory.

Their mother always decorated the tree and they were never allowed to see it until the candles were lit. That year the tree stood in the small annexe to the drawing-room – a perfect place, because there were curtains which could be drawn back when the tree was to be seen in all its glory. That year there were about fifteen people, mostly women, all rather shy and sad while they drank tea and ate Victoria's birthday – now the Christmas – cake.

When the tea was cleared, Annie and Hester joined the party, and soon everyone was circling the tree singing *The First Nowell* and then *Good King Wenceslas*, with John singing the King's verses and Victoria the page's. Then came the time to strip the tree. The majority of the parcels were for the family of course, but no one was allowed to feel left out, so there were plenty of little gifts for the guests. Annie and Hester (Miss Herbert went to a brother for Christmas) had presents from every member of the family and, as well as proper presents from the children's parents, each received an afternoon apron. Annie said when she opened her parcel:

'Thank you, madam. It will save you buying me one for when you want me to bring in tea on Hester's day out.'

The present-giving over and the wrappings swept up, the charades started and, as had been hoped, Mr Plimsol proved a natural comic. It was lovely to see the lonely, rather sad people who had arrived, mopping the tears of laughter off their cheeks.

Then there was more carol singing and then the guests were in the hall putting on their wraps, and another Christmas Day was over.

How We Lived Then

NORMAN LONGMATE

During the Second World War, those 'dull grey years of bombs, blackouts and rationing', any kind of celebration was difficult, but the biggest challenge of all was Christmas. This account draws on the experience of a number of different people. There were some strange Christmas dinners in those days, but every- one tried to make Christmas special for the children.

For an Oldham schoolgirl the privations of wartime were summed up in her family's Christmas dinner in 1944: mutton pie followed by 'wartime Christmas pudding', made with grated carrots. (The official recipes also suggested grated apples and chopped prunes and dried elderberries to replace the missing dried fruit. The results were rarely very palatable to those old enough to remember the real thing.) One Manchester woman had even more reason than most to remember the great blitz of December 1940, for 'my mother's house in Didsbury had had a direct hit *and* my mother-in-law's house in Chorlton and they all descended on me in my little flat. Our Christmas dinner consisted of corned beef hash and wartime Christmas pudding, but we listened to the wireless, sang, played cards and generally had a good time'.

Christmas cards were still sent during the war though most mantelpieces contained more 'official' cards with coats of arms, from the Women's Land Army to the Home Guard, than stage-coaches and snow scenes. A few patriotic people made their own cards by stencilling designs on newspaper, but this was generally felt to be carrying austerity too far.

One might, if fortunate, find a Christmas tree, though one mother still remembers with regret that her child never had the joy of seeing a Christmas tree decorated with electric lights, but decorations of some kind could be improvised and one Essex woman's 'happiest memory' is of 'sitting for hours with my small son making flowers and stars from silver paper to put on an otherwise empty Christmas tree'. Painted egg-shells and fir-cones, and fragments of silver paper from processed cheese packets, were also used as decorations, 'angels' and 'fairy dolls' were made from stiff paper and the blue packets in which cotton wool was sold were opened out and cut into strips for paper chains. Crackers were usually missing, but one East Ham family even succeeded in producing a version of their own, from the cardboard centres of toilet rolls, wrapped in crêpe paper, with, inside each, a home-made paper hat and a fire-cracker left over from Home Guard exercises.

Few Christmas stockings were left unfilled despite the war. A Sheffield girl, two when the war began, eight when it finished, remembers asking in her letter to Santa Claus for 'any little thing you can spare'. 'This touched my mother,' she says, '– but at the time I couldn't see why. It just seemed logical.' A Surrey girl, six in 1939, remembers being put to bed one Christmas Eve in the shelter in the cellar and leaving detailed instructions on the dining room table to Santa Claus, lest he fail to locate this unconventional bedroom. A Liverpool woman remembers how another little girl was made happy that year despite the war:

'Christmas 1941. The men were away, except my elder brother who had served in the First World War and was in the Home Guard. My daughter had asked Father Christmas for a doll's house. We looked at each other in dismay. Then my brother found an old birdcage. During the raids he worked on it: found bits of cardboard for the walls. The office wastepaper basket provided an old file which made the roof. He painted the floors. We hunted for all kinds of bits and pieces and a miracle was achieved... A piece of hessian, dyed red, fringed, made an elegant carpet. Never will I forget her face that dark Christmas morning and her childish voice piping "There'll be blue birds over the white cliffs of Dover" as she saw those tables and chairs, tiny pictures made out of cigarette cards, her cries of joy as she discovered each new thing.'

On the whole, very small children probably came off best. Rag dolls, with button eyes, could fairly readily be made from old stockings, old coats could be converted into stuffed animals, seaboot stockings, unravelled, could be reknitted as teddy bears and in one family in Somerset, an old pair of grey flannel trousers proved the basis for a pull-along elephant. Keen toy-makers hoarded every scrap of material, if not for sewing outside then for stuffing within; one family even saved the small plugs of cotton wool in the tops of aspirin bottles. Cardboard milk bottle tops and large buttons provided the mechanism of 'whizzers', which whirred round when their supporting strings were jerked tight, and in one Yorkshire factory toy-hungry fathers discovered that its basic product, round door-knobs, could serve a new use as yo-yos. A Birmingham builder, posted to London to help in repairs during the flying bomb raids, remembers that his workmates and himself 'made kaleidoscopes in our spare time, using bits of tinfoil, chips of coloured broken glass, etc.', and one mother, evacuated to Exeter with two small girls, brightened their Christmases with cardboard snowmen made from empty Vim canisters, covered with cotton wool and with a black circle of card for a hat, filled 'with little trinkets, sweets, etc. and perhaps an orange'.

Despite all their parents' efforts, many children did miss some of the customary pleasures during the war. One mother still feels sad that her daughter's only dolls were of the cardboard type, with cut-out clothes: the normal china type were simply beyond her means. Inevitably, too, the war deprived children of the pleasure of spending their pocket money as they wished. A Hawick, Roxburghshire, woman witnessed its effects on one small boy in 1944. He had called into the village Post Office to buy a comic but was told 'They haven't come in this week'. He then asked for sweets, and was told 'No sweeties either' and, after a further question, 'Not even chewing gum'. At this, he asked for a penny stamp, walked out and stuck it on the pillar box outside, remarking 'That Hitler!'

The Christmas in Mama's Kitchen

JEAN BELL MOSLEY

For years, we put the Christmas tree in the parlor. It was the fanciest room in the old farmhouse – carpeted, wallpapered, and curtained. It seemed fitting to celebrate the Master's birthday in the best room.

However, there was too much activity going on from day to day in the big kitchen – Mama's kitchen – to maintain an unused fire elsewhere, so there wasn't always a fire burning in the parlor. Grandma and Mama cooked, sewed, churned, washed, and ironed in the kitchen. Dad and Grandpa kept their accounts, read the papers, soled shoes there. My two sisters and I did homework, helped with the chores, played our games there. Mama's kitchen fireplace was always aglow, the range constantly fired. It was a big spacious room – bright and cozy.

On December Sundays or special holidays, when company was expected, Dad would make a fire in the parlor stove and we'd all go in to enjoy the tree, breathe its cedary fragrance, touch the old familiar baubles. Baby Jesus, in his crib in the crèche beneath the tree, would, after a long time, feel warm to our touch.

But somehow the parlor never had the coziness Mama's kitchen had. I always liked the big center table we gathered around, face to face, making small talk or sometimes serious talk. If Mama read a Christmas story aloud in the parlor, it wasn't the same as in the kitchen accompanied by the sputtering fireplace and singing teakettle. Even our evening prayers seemed to come naturally in the kitchen.

One winter evening, as the fire died in the parlor stove, I boldly lifted the crib from the crèche and took it into the kitchen, setting it near the fireplace. My sisters, thinking I had been irreverent, told Mama.

'Let it be,' Mama said. She smiled at me, though I had expected a reprimand.

The next Christmas, when Dad and Grandpa brought the tree

home, Mama said, 'I mean to put it up here in the kitchen this year.'

'Celebrate His birthday in here with the smell of cabbage cooking, the butter being churned, our old barn clothes hanging over there?' one of my sisters demanded.

'Let's try it,' Mama said.

The hat rack was moved a little closer to the sewing machine. The cot was pushed up against another wall to make room. When we came downstairs for breakfast, in from the outdoor chores, home from school, there was the tree, bright, warm, and fragrant. We trimmed it leisurely – cranberry chains one evening, popcorn garlands the next. Baby Jesus, in the crib, close and dear, was always warm, as were the little sheep, donkeys, shepherds, and Wise Men.

When we read the Christmas story, starting seven nights before Christmas so each could have his turn at reading it, the event that happened so long ago and far away now seemed so close, as if it might have happened just last night in our own cow stable. I could visualize the Baby lying in Star's haylined feed box; hear the soft, velvety whinny of Dobbin looking on through the bars; the stirrings of other creatures that had come in from the cold.

The moon and stars that the shepherds saw that night in their pastures were the same moon and stars that shone on me when I went to close the chicken-house door. White-bearded Grandpa, coming in from the snowy outdoors, bearing a gift of shiny red apples from the apple hole, looked very much like a Wise Man. We didn't know what had happened to our Christmas, but we knew it was better than any we'd ever had.

One afternoon a neighbor dropped in with some cookies. 'Why, Myrtle,' she said to Mama, 'is this – is – this – appropriate – ?' Her voice trailed off. But after looking around the kitchen her face lit up. 'Myrtle,' she exclaimed, 'you've brought Christmas in here to be an everyday thing, warm and comfortable, right amongst your living!'

Mama smiled and replied, 'Only our best for the Master.' She may have winked at me. I don't know. Fireplace shadows sometimes play tricks, and holiday eyes get so bright they have to blink often.

7
The Christmas Play

For many people, Christmas begins with the nativity play, as children – and grown-ups – re-enact the story of Mary and Joseph, the baby Jesus, the coming of the shepherds and the three Wise Men.
The stories in this section are all about putting on the Christmas play, and the dramas, horrors, tears, laughter and fun which surround it.

Nativity Play

CLARE BEVAN

Here is an inn with a stable,
Equipped with some straw and a chair.
Here is an angel in bed sheets,
with tinsel to tie back her hair.

Here is a servant in bath towels
Who sweeps round the stage with a broom.
Here is a chorus of faces
All eager to cry out, 'NO ROOM!'

Here is a Joseph who stammers,
And tries to remember his lines.
Here is a teacher in anguish,
Who frantically gestures and signs.

Here is 'Away In A Manger' –
A tune MOST recorders can play.
Here is the moment of wonder,
As Jesus appears in the hay.

Here is a Mary with freckles
Whose baby is plastic and hard.
Here is a donkey in trousers,
With ears made from pieces of card.

Here is a shepherd in curtains,
Who carries a crook made of wire.
Here is a boy sucking cough sweets,
Who growls from the back of the choir.

Here is a King bearing bath salts,
Who points at a star hung on strings.
Here is a dove who has stage fright,
And quivers her crêpe-paper wings.

Here is a page boy in plimsolls
Who stumbles his way up the stairs.
Here is a long line of cherubs
Who march round the manger in pairs.

Here is a camel who fidgets,
With plasters stuck over his knee.
Here are some sheep who just giggle,
And think no one out there can see.

Here is a Herod in glasses
Who whispers, so nobody hears.
Here is a Mum with a hanky,
To cover her pride and her tears.

Here is our final production,
And though it's still held up with pins,
The parents will love every minute –
For this is where Christmas begins.

The First Rehearsal

From *The Best Christmas Pageant Ever/The Worst Kids in the World*

BARBARA ROBINSON

*The Herdmans were so all-round awful you could hardly
believe they were real: Ralph, Imogene, Leroy, Claude, Ollie
and Gladys – six skinny, stringy-haired kids all alike except for
being different sizes.
So when they got the lead parts in the Christmas pageant there
was bound to be trouble. Yet this turned out to be the best
Christmas pageant ever!*

The first pageant rehearsal was usually about as much fun as a
three-hour ride on the school bus, and just as noisy and crowded.
This rehearsal, though, was different. Everybody shut up and settled
down right away, for fear of missing something awful that the
Herdmans might do.

They got there ten minutes late, sliding into the room like a
bunch of outlaws about to shoot up a saloon. When Leroy passed
Charlie he knuckled him behind the ear, and one little primary girl
yelled as Gladys went by. But Mother had said she was going to
ignore everything except blood, and since the primary kid wasn't
bleeding, and neither was Charlie, nothing happened.

Mother said, 'And here's the Herdman family. We're glad to see
you all,' which was probably the biggest lie ever said out loud in
the church.

Imogene smiled – the Herdman smile, we called it, sly and
sneaky – and there they sat, the closest thing to criminals that we
knew about, and they were going to represent the best and most
beautiful. No wonder everybody was so worked up.

Mother started to separate everyone into angels and shepherds
and guests at the inn, but right away she ran into trouble.

'Who were the shepherds?' Leroy Herdman wanted to know.
'Where did they come from?'

Ollie Herdman didn't even know what a shepherd was... or,

anyway, that's what he said.

'What was the inn?' Claude asked. 'What's an inn?'

'It's like a motel,' somebody told him, 'where people go to spend the night.'

'What people?' Claude said. 'Jesus?'

'Oh, honestly!' Alice Wendleken grumbled. 'Jesus wasn't even born yet! Mary and Joseph went there.'

'Why?' Ralph asked.

'What happened first?' Imogene hollered at my mother. 'Begin at the beginning!'

That really scared me because the beginning would be the Book of Genesis, where it says 'In the beginning...' and if we were going to have to start with the Book of Genesis we'd never get through.

The thing was, the Herdmans didn't know anything about the Christmas story. They knew that Christmas was Jesus' birthday, but everything else was news to them – the shepherds, the Wise Men, the star, the stable, the crowded inn.

It was hard to believe... but they just didn't know. And Mother said she had better begin by reading the Christmas story from the Bible. This was a pain in the neck to most of us because we knew the whole thing backward and forward and never had to be told anything except who we were supposed to be, and where we were supposed to stand.

'...Joseph and Mary, his espoused wife, being great with child...'

'Pregnant!' yelled Ralph Herdman.

Well. That stirred things up. All the big kids began to giggle and all the little kids wanted to know what was so funny, and Mother had to hammer on the floor with a blackboard pointer. 'That's enough, Ralph,' she said, and went on with the story.

'I don't think it's very nice to say Mary was pregnant,' Alice whispered to me.

'But she was,' I pointed out. In a way, though, I agreed with her. It sounded too ordinary. Anybody could be pregnant. 'Great with child' sounded better for Mary.

'I'm not supposed to talk about people being pregnant.' Alice folded her hands in her lap and pinched her lips together. 'I'd better tell my mother.'

'Tell her what?'

'That your mother is talking about things like that in church. My mother might not want me to be here.'

I was pretty sure she would do it. She wanted to be Mary, and she was mad at Mother. I knew, too, that she would make it sound worse than it was and Mrs Wendleken would get madder than she already was. Mrs Wendleken didn't even want cats to have kittens or birds to lay eggs, and she wouldn't let Alice play with anybody who had two rabbits.

But there wasn't much I could do about it, except pinch Alice, which I did. She yelped, and Mother separated us and made me sit beside Imogene Herdman and sent Alice to sit in the middle of the baby angels.

I wasn't crazy to sit next to Imogene – after all, I'd spent my whole life staying away from Imogene – but she didn't even notice me... not much, anyway.

'Shut up,' was all she said. 'I want to hear her.'

I couldn't believe it. Among other things, the Herdmans were famous for never sitting still and never paying attention to anyone – teachers, parents (their own or anybody else's), the truant officer, the police – yet here they were, eyes glued on my mother and taking in every word.

'What's that?' they would yell whenever they didn't understand the language, and when Mother read about there being no room at the inn, Imogene's jaw dropped and she sat up in her seat.

'My God!' she said. 'Not even for Jesus?'

I saw Alice purse her lips together so I knew that was something else Mrs Wendleken would hear about – swearing in the church.

'Well, now, after all,' Mother explained, 'nobody knew the baby was going to turn out to be Jesus.'

'You said Mary knew,' Ralph said. 'Why didn't she tell them?'

'I would have told them!' Imogene put in. 'Boy, would I have told them! What was the matter with Joseph that he didn't tell them? Her pregnant and everything,' she grumbled.

'What was that they laid the baby in?' Leroy said. 'That manger... is that like a bed? Why would they have a bed in the barn?'

'That's just the point,' Mother said. 'They *didn't* have a bed in the barn, so Mary and Joseph had to use whatever there was. What would you do if you have a new baby and no bed to put the baby in?'

'We put Gladys in a bureau drawer,' Imogene volunteered.

'Well, there you are,' Mother said, blinking a little. 'You didn't have a bed for Gladys so you had to use something else.'

'Oh, we had a bed,' Ralph said, 'only Ollie was still in it and he wouldn't get out. He didn't like Gladys.' He elbowed Ollie. 'Remember how you didn't like Gladys?'

I thought that was pretty smart of Ollie, not to like Gladys right off the bat.

'*Anyway*,' Mother said, 'Mary and Joseph used the manger. A manger is a large wooden feeding trough for animals.'

'What were the wadded-up clothes?' Claude wanted to know.

'The what?' Mother said.

'You read about it – "she wrapped him in wadded-up clothes."'

'*Swaddling* clothes.' Mother sighed. 'Long ago, people used to wrap their babies very tightly in big pieces of material, so they couldn't move around. It made the babies feel cosy and comfortable.'

I thought it probably just made the babies mad. Till then, I didn't know what swaddling clothes were either, and they sounded terrible, so I wasn't too surprised when Imogene got all excited about that.

'You mean they tied him up and put him in a feedbox?' she said. 'Where was the Child Welfare?'

The Child Welfare was always checking up on the Herdmans. I'll bet if the Child Welfare had ever found Gladys all tied up in a bureau drawer they would have done something about it.

'And, lo, the Angel of the Lord came upon them,' Mother went on, 'and the glory of the Lord shone round about them, and – '

'Shazam!' Gladys yelled, flinging her arms out and smacking the kid next to her.

'What?' Mother said. Mother never read 'Amazing Comics'.

'Out of the black night with horrible vengeance, the Mighty Marvo – '

'I don't know what you're talking about, Gladys,' Mother said. 'This is the Angel of the Lord who comes to the shepherds in the fields, and – '

'Out of nowhere, right?' Gladys said. 'In the black night, right?'

'Well...' Mother looked unhappy. 'In a way.'

So Gladys sat back down, looking very satisfied, as if this was at least one part of the Christmas story that made sense to her.

'Now when Jesus was born in Bethlehem of Judaea,' Mother went on reading, 'behold there came Wise Men from the East to Jerusalem, saying – '

'That's you, Leroy,' Ralph said, 'and Claude and Ollie. So pay attention.'

'What does it mean, Wise Men?' Ollie wanted to know. 'Were they like schoolteachers?'

'No, dumbbell,' Claude said. 'It means like President of the United States.'

Mother looked surprised, and a little pleased – like she did when Charlie finally learned the times-tables up to five. 'Why, that's very close, Claude,' she said. 'Actually, they were kings.'

'Well, it's about time,' Imogene muttered. 'Maybe they'll tell the innkeeper where to get off, and get the baby out of the barn.'

'They saw the young child with Mary, his mother, and fell down and worshipped him, and presented unto him gifts: gold, and frankincense, and myrrh.'

'What's that stuff?' Leroy wanted to know.

'Precious oils,' Mother said, 'and fragrant resins.'

'Oil!' Imogene hollered. 'What kind of a cheap king hands out oil for a present? You get better presents from the firemen!'

Sometimes the Herdmans got Christmas presents at the Firemen's Party, but the Santa Claus always had to feel all around the packages to be sure they weren't getting bows and arrows or dart guns or anything like that. Imogene usually got sewing cards or jigsaw puzzles and she never liked them, but I guess she figured they were better than oil.

Then we came to King Herod, and the Herdmans never heard of him either, so Mother had to explain that it was Herod who sent the Wise Men to find the baby Jesus.

'Was it him that sent the crummy presents?' Ollie wanted to know, and Mother said it was worse than that – he planned to have the baby Jesus put to death.

'My God!' Imogene said. 'He just got born and already they're out to kill him!'

The Herdmans wanted to know all about Herod – what he looked like, and how rich he was, and whether he fought wars with people.

'He must have been the main king,' Claude said, 'if he could make the other three do what he wanted them to.'

'If I was a king,' Leroy said, 'I wouldn't let some other king push me around.'

'You couldn't help it if he was the main king.'

'I'd go be king somewhere else.'

They were really interested in Herod, and I figured they liked him. He was so mean he could have been their ancestor – Herod Herdman. But I was wrong.

'Who's going to be Herod in this play?' Leroy said.

'We don't show Herod in our pageant,' Mother said. And they all got mad. They wanted somebody to be Herod so they could beat up on him.

I couldn't understand the Herdmans. You would have thought the Christmas story came right out of the F.B.I. files, they got so involved in it – wanted a bloody end to Herod, worried about Mary having her baby in a barn, and called the Wise Men a bunch of dirty spies.

And they left the first rehearsal arguing about whether Joseph should have set fire to the inn, or just chased the innkeeper into the next county.

If

JANEY MITSON (AGED 9)

If I were a shepherd
That the Angels came to see,
To tell me of a new birth,
That would mean the world to me.

Would I have taken my best lamb
That was perhaps a whole week's pay,
And given it to a baby,
That was born on Christmas Day?

Would I have really believed
What the Angels said was true,
That this little baby was God's only son,
I'm not sure I would, are you?

If I were a wise man
Would I have gone so far,
With nothing more to guide me,
But a shining star?

I've never seen an angel
Or such a shining star,
I've never ridden a camel,
Or travelled very far.

But I have read my Bible
And I know the story's true,
That Jesus came from heaven,
For me and also you.

Trouble at the Inn

DINA DONOHUE

For years now whenever Christmas pageants are talked about in a certain little town in the Midwest, someone is sure to mention the name of Wallace Purling.

Wally's performance in one annual production of the nativity play has slipped into the realm of legend. But the old-timers who were in the audience that night never tire of recalling exactly what happened.

Wally was nine that year and in the second grade, though he should have been in the fourth. Most people in town knew that he had difficulty in keeping up. He was big and clumsy, slow in movement and mind. Still, Wally was well liked by the other children in his class, all of whom were smaller than he, though the boys had trouble hiding their irritation when Wally would ask to play ball with them or any game, for that matter, in which winning was important.

Most often they'd find a way to keep him out, but Wally would hang around anyway – not sulking, just hoping. He was always a helpful boy, a willing and smiling one, and the natural protector, paradoxically, of the underdog. If the older boys chased the younger ones away, it would always be Wally who'd say, 'Can't they stay? They're no bother.'

Wally fancied the idea of being a shepherd with a flute in the Christmas pageant that year, but the play's director, Miss Lumbard, assigned him to a more important role. After all, she reasoned, the Innkeeper did not have too many lines, and Wally's size would make his refusal of lodging to Joseph more forceful.

And so it happened that the usual large, partisan audience gathered for the town's yearly extravaganza of crooks and crèches, of beards, crowns, halos, and a whole stage full of squeaky voices. No one on stage or off was more caught up in the magic of the night than Wallace Purling. They said later that he stood in the wings and watched the performance with such fascination that

145

from time to time Miss Lumbard had to make sure he didn't wander onstage before his cue.

Then the time came when Joseph appeared, slowly, tenderly guiding Mary to the door of the inn. Joseph knocked hard on the wooden door set into the painted backdrop. Wally the Innkeeper was there, waiting.

'What do you want?' Wally said, swinging the door open with a brusque gesture.

'We seek lodging.'

'Seek it elsewhere.' Wally looked straight ahead but spoke vigorously. 'The inn is filled.'

'Sir, we have asked everywhere in vain. We have travelled far and are very weary.'

'There is no room in this inn for you.' Wally looked properly stern.

'Please, good Innkeeper, this is my wife, Mary. She is heavy with child and needs a place to rest. Surely you must have some small corner for her. She is so tired.'

Now, for the first time, the Innkeeper relaxed his stiff stance and looked down at Mary. With that, there was a long pause, long enough to make the audience a bit tense with embarrassment.

'No! Begone!' the prompter whispered from the wings.

'No!' Wally repeated automatically. 'Begone!'

Joseph sadly placed his arm around Mary, and Mary laid her head upon her husband's shoulder, and the two of them started to move away. The Innkeeper did not return inside his inn, however. Wally stood there in the doorway, watching the forlorn couple. His mouth was open, his brow creased with concern, his eyes filling unmistakably with tears.

And suddenly this Christmas pageant became different from all others.

'Don't go, Joseph,' Wally called out. 'Bring Mary back.' And Wallace Purling's face grew into a bright smile. 'You can have my room.'

Some people in town thought that the pageant had been ruined. Yet there were others – many, many others – who considered it the most Christmas of all Christmas pageants they had ever seen.

One Stupid Line

From *Chris and the Dragon*

FAY SAMPSON

*Chris is never out of trouble. But when he's chosen to be
Joseph in the school nativity play he really tries to be good. It's
just bad luck that he leans his weight on the curtain, and
brings the whole thing, pole and all, down on the stage.
Thanks to this, Mrs Maltby gives the part to his best friend
Tuan. Instead Chris is playing the innkeeper, with just one
line to say...*

Chris felt sick. His mum was coming to school today for the first
time. To see him. To watch him being Joseph in the Christmas
play. For once in his life she thought he'd done something really
good. She'd told the whole street. She was bringing Gran.

He couldn't tell her. He didn't know how to tell her that he'd
made a mess of it. That he wasn't going to be Joseph any more.
Just the innkeeper. One line to say. One stupid line. He had to
shake his head, and tell them there was no room at the inn, and
shut the door. And that was him finished. The rest of the play
would go on without him. She was wasting her time, coming to
see him just do that.

'You don't *have* to come. It's not important.'

'Of course we're coming.'

He crawled away to school. He looked into the hall and scowled
at the rows of empty seats. The innkeeper's part wasn't worth
bothering with. You could learn a part like that in five seconds.
He'd rather not be in the play at all now. He even wondered about
running away.

But he was still there when they started dressing up for the
play. At least he still had his Joseph costume, with the red and
gold stripes. He had tried Tuan's costume, but it only came down
to his knees. And the red and gold Joseph gown fell over Tuan like
a collapsed parachute. So Mr Downes had said they had better

147

keep their own.

They were all ready. The curtains at the front of the stage were shut. Chris was waiting at the back, hidden behind the inn door. He could hear the chatter from the hall.

Then he saw Mr Downes give the signal. The curtains opened. Tuan was standing in the middle of the stage, where Chris should have been. And all the mums went, 'Aah!'

Somewhere out there in the hall, Chris's mum would be sitting with Gran. Looking at Joseph. Seeing it wasn't Chris. Wondering what had gone wrong. She'd told all her friends he was going to be Joseph.

He peeped through the crack in the inn door, and backed away. The school hall was full of people. Rows and rows of mums and dads and little brothers and sisters. And in the front row, Mrs Maltby, smiling at the vicar, and a lot of men in small grey suits and ladies in posh coats and Sunday hats.

That Mrs Maltby. He'd get her some day. It was all her fault.

Joseph and Mary and the donkey were getting nearer. Any moment now, they'd be knocking at the door. Any moment now, he'd have to say his one silly line.

'No, every room is full. Be off. You heard what I said.'

And that would be it. Finished. The play would go on without him, and all the interesting things would start to happen. That was what the other mums were waiting for.

Lisa would pick Sally's doll out of the manger, and Lisa's mum would go, 'Aah!'

The angels would come trooping on in their white robes, and the angels' mums would go, 'Aah!'

The shepherds would come with their lambs, and the shepherds' mums would go, 'Aah!'

The kings would come in their bright robes and crowns, and the kings' mums would go, 'Aah!'

But all Chris's mum would see was Chris shaking his head and shutting the door. Nobody would go 'Aah!' about that.

Tuan knocked at the inn door. Chris heard it, but he didn't think anyone else would. So he knocked noisily himself, from the inside. Then he opened the door and stood there for everyone to see. Nobody said anything this time. They just waited.

Little Tuan smiled up at him and asked, *'Please have you any room for us? My wife must have a bed.'*

And he stood there, smiling and waiting.

Everyone was waiting now. Waiting for Chris. Waiting for him to say there was no room at the inn. Waiting for the play to go on. And Chris began to smile too. Maybe it didn't have to be such a silly part, after all.

He looked down at the hall. They were all waiting. Mrs Maltby and the governors in their posh suits. The ladies in silly hats. The vicar. The mums and dads and grans, and little brothers and sisters. The teachers in the back row.

All waiting for Chris. Waiting for him to shake his head and shut the door. Waiting for all the best bits to start. For the stable, and the angels, and the shepherds, and the kings.

Tuan had stopped smiling now. He began to whisper the inn-keeper's words to Chris.

Chris smiled down at him kindly. He hadn't forgotten his line. But he wasn't going to say it now. An idea was growing in his mind. It was a lovely idea.

He smiled at Mrs Maltby and all the people in the hall. Just a little smile at first. But the smile got wider and wider. He smiled at Tuan's yellow face and Lisa's black one, till he was beaming a huge, happy, glorious welcome to them.

Then, with a flourish, he threw the inn door open as wide as it would go. He pointed inside and said in a ringing voice,

'Room? Of course we've got room. *Hundreds* of rooms! It's Christmas, isn't it? Come in and make yourselves welcome, mate!'

149

There was a deathly silence.

And then the vicar began to laugh. And the men in Sunday suits began to laugh, and the ladies in hats, and the mums and dads and little brothers and sisters. The teachers in the back row were creasing themselves with laughter. And they were all standing up and clapping and cheering fit to bring the roof down, as Chris swept Tuan and Lisa into the inn and shut the door behind them.

Christmas Joy

HELEN ROBINSON (AGED 13)

The audience, chilled from the frosty night
Fumbled into the stuffy hall.
Silver stars clung,
Tinsel was drooped around the crammed room.
They sat, not knowing what to expect
From a group of children wearing old curtains
And tinsel round their heads.
The hall grew warmer,
A light beamed on to a home-made crib.
A cloth was draped over Jesus' worn face.
Backstage everyone was excited,
Except me.
Hot and clammy, I sat in a corner
Waiting for my turn.
I was pushed on to the stage
And blinded.
My angel's costume was crumpled,
My face was numb.
I could see the Headmaster
Lounging in his plastic chair.
He gave a smile,
Urging me to speak.
One eye gave a friendly wink.
It was Christmas.

The Gypsy Christmas Play

From *Nowhere to Stop*

GERALDINE KAYE

*Liberty and Pattella Lovell – two gypsy children – have joined
the class at Wood Lane School. Pattella is playing Mary in the
Christmas play. When people want to move the gypsies on,
Chris tries to help, but things get muddled. (Julie is one of the
grown-ups on the gypsies' side, trying to find a place for
them.) But perhaps the Christmas play has something to say
about people with nowhere to stop.*

In the cloakroom of Wood Lane School it was dress rehearsal for
the Christmas play. Everybody was helping because they'd only got
till tomorrow. In one corner Mr Beach in his yellow shirt was going
over scene two with the shepherds. In the inn Tom was trying to
teach his guests to sing *Lavender blue dilly dilly*, like Miss Lee said,
only the guests said it was a soppy song.

Miss Lee was sticking gold paper crowns for the three kings,
and June was putting fruit gum jewels on them. Dusty and Ron
were practising the donkey and the 'Blues' were practising *Hark the
Herald Angels Sing*.

Chris sat by himself. He was miserable; nobody would talk to
him and, anyway, Julie knew the Gypsies were on the airfield and
Liberty would think Chris had told and he hadn't and it wasn't
fair.

Feet came hurrying down the stone stairs. It was Liberty in his
cowboy hat and Pattella with a great basket of Christmas flowers
on her arm, and Julie. There was silence and then everybody was
shouting with excitement.

'Pattella for Mary.'

'Where you Gypsies got to?' Ron shouted...

'Get into your Mary costume, Pattella,' Mr Beach said, and
Chris fetched the blue curtain.

'I didn't tell where you were, honest, I didn't,' he whispered,

152

but Pattella neither cared nor understood the Gaujo boy. She pushed the cushion inside her cardigan. 'You don't need that for scene three, silly,' June said.

Julie turned to Miss Lee. 'I wonder if I can help? I have helped with plays before.'

'We need all the help we can get with this one,' said Miss Lee crisply, as she stuck the last jewel on the last crown. Chris edged his way across to Liberty.

'I didn't tell, honest, I didn't,' he whispered urgently.

'We're going on with scene three,' Mr Beach said, and Pattella sat in the centre of the stage with the blue curtain and the African blanket over her head, and Chris stood behind her. They had a wooden box for the manger now and real straw, that Linda was going to take home for her hamster, but they only had a bundle of overalls for the baby. Suddenly Mary said, 'Pattella can have my baby Jesus.' Everybody clapped and Mary passed the baby doll to Chris.

'Thanks,' he whispered, and he put it in the manger. Mary got up on her chair and shone the bright star right on to baby Jesus...

Julie was taking the red Christmas flowers out of the basket and putting them round the baby Jesus in the manger. 'It's a Gypsy Christmas play isn't it?' she said.

'Looks pretty,' said June.

'Lovely,' said Rosie.

'Cost you,' Liberty said.

'How much?' said Miss Lee. 'We have a little money for the Christmas play.'

'One pound to you, lady,' Liberty said in a wheedling tone. 'You gotta lucky face, lady.'

'You coming to the Christmas play?' asked Chris's sister, June. The warm kitchen smelt of sardines on toast. June packed her mouth as full as she could and then picked up her knitting needles and cast on a new blue square.

'Don't know about your dad,' said Mum.

'Can't get off work three o'clock, can I?' said Dad.

'I'll ask Nan,' said Mum. 'Pity to waste the ticket.'

'We got this Gypsy girl for Mary,' said Chris.

'Bit funny, isn't it?' said Mum. 'A Gypsy for Mary?'

153

'What's funny?' said Chris. 'Mary and Joseph had black hair and they didn't have anywhere to stop.'

It was almost three o'clock. The 'Reds' were showing people to their places. The hall was full of people all whispering and chattering, except for the front row which was being kept for Mr Page and the people from the Council. Chris twisted the striped stuff round his head. Could they tell if the signatures in his letter were real? Suppose one of the Council was to stand up and ask him about it when he was being Joseph?

'There's our mum, second row back,' said Rosie, peeping through the stage curtains.

'There's our Nan,' said Chris.

'Where?' said June, and she knelt down and looked underneath, and there was Mum and Nan in her new green coat. June was prompter; she sat on the edge of the stage and reminded people who forgot their words. Liberty sat beside her, writing his name and scowling because Mr Beach wouldn't let him sit under the Christmas tree.

Everything was ready. Behind the curtain Pattella and Chris waited with the donkey for scene one. Only the donkey kept fidgeting, and Chris's throat felt rather dry. Mr Beach had on his moss-green shirt and there were beads of sweat on his forehead. Miss Lee sat at the piano and rubbed her swollen hands together...

Ma Lovell stood in the doorway. She had Hopsy under one arm and a big basket of Christmas flowers on the other. She didn't like this shut-in Gaujo place. Still it was no different from the market really with its glass roof. She swung the basket and walked towards the front row.

'Buy my Christmas flowers? Five pence each. Twenty-five for a bunch of six.' The hall was quiet; everybody stared, and Hopsy put his thumb in his mouth and stared back.

'Oh dear,' said Miss Lee. 'Liberty, I really don't think...'

Liberty pulled his hat down and scowled. Ma Lovell sat down in the front row and put a bunch of Christmas flowers on Mrs White's navy-blue lap.

'Only twenty-five pence, lady. You got a lucky face, lady,' she said, and then the Chairman of the Council came in, with a big gold medal on a chain. There were several other men in dark suits, and ladies with flowery hats and smiles. They all sat down in the front row with Mr Page.

'Lights,' shouted Mr Beach. 'Curtains.'

Suddenly it was dark and absolutely quiet, and then Miss Lee played a chord and the 'Reds' started singing *The Holly and the Ivy*, and the curtains slid open and Mr Page said, 'It's rather an experiment.'

Chris's mouth was dry as sand. Had they read his letter? He stared at the faces round as moons, and he couldn't speak.

'Us is ever so tired,' Pattella shouted. She liked all the Gaujé watching her, and she leaned on Chris's arm and limped forward and pulled at the donkey. At first the donkey just stood still, twitching.

It was the hiccups, Dusty said after.

Then the donkey lurched forward. 'Us is ever so tired. Mary is tired,' Pattella shouted, and she gave Chris a hard pinch and he began to speak. 'My poor wife, Mary, is tired, ever so tired,' he said. At first his voice sounded like a key turned in a rusty lock but then it sounded better.

The play went well until Chris said 'There is an inn. Perhaps we can stay there. I'll go and knock.' The knock was the signal for the singing to start in the inn. Some of the guests sang *Lavender blue dilly dilly*, and some sang *The Holly and the Ivy*, and some sang *Roll out the Barrel* because that's what people sang at The Bull.

'Stop that,' Tom whispered, and he pushed his guests. 'Stop that.' Tom went very pink because his mum was just there in the front row. He forgot what he was meant to say, so he didn't say anything.

'I'll go and knock,' Chris said, rather more loudly. He knocked on the bench with his fist and Tom went white, but he still couldn't think what he was *meant* to say and so he said, 'Who's that knocking?'

'You don't say that,' whispered June.

'It's us,' said Chris. 'It's Joseph and Mary. We're poor people and my wife is ever so tired and we've got nowhere to stop.'

Tom just stood there because he still couldn't remember what to say, and June said in a loud whisper. 'There's no room here. The inn is full.'

'There's no room here. The inn is full,' said Tom.

'May we sleep in your stable?' Chris said.

'Let them sleep with the animals,' said one of the guests, and the others started singing different songs again, and Tom said, 'Stop that.'

'May we sleep in your stable?' said Chris.

'No,' said Tom. 'Go away.'

Chris couldn't go away because Mary and Joseph *had* to sleep in the stable. So he knocked again and said, 'May we sleep in your stable?'

'No...' stammered Tom.

'May we sleep in your stable?' said Chris for the third time, and his voice was rather high and squeaky.

'No,' stammered Tom. 'No.'

'You got to let them,' June whispered.

'Show them the stable, Tom,' Mr Beach said quite loudly, and all round the hall there was whispering.

'May we sleep in your stable?' Chris shouted, and Pattella threw herself on the ground with a loud wailing moan. Everybody in the audience was quiet at once and something clicked in Tom's head.

'All right, I'll get my lantern and show you the way,' he said.

All round the hall there was a great sigh of relief. Tom took Mary and Joseph to the stable and the curtains closed for the end of scene one.

'Buy my Christmas flowers, lady?' said Ma Lovell loudly.

'Certainly not,' said Mrs White with her lips very tight.

'Hold 'un then,' said Ma Lovell, and she put Hopsy on to Mrs White's lap and walked along the front row with her basket. 'Buy us Christmas flowers? Five pence each or a bunch for twenty-five,' she shouted.

'Well, I really don't think we...' Mr Page began, but one of the ladies said, 'They really are beautiful. Most unusual.' She took twenty-five pence from her handbag.

'You've got a lucky face, lady,' Ma Lovell said.

Then it was time for scene two, and Miss Lee played *While Shepherds Watched their Flocks* and the curtains opened. The three shepherds sat round their flashing red fire that was really Linda and the torch. Ma Lovell waited till the curtains closed again and then she shouted, 'Christmas flowers. Lovely bunch for twenty-five pence.' She sold several bunches and got back to her place just in time for scene three.

'Where's my Hopsy?' she said.

'Hush,' whispered Mrs White. 'He wouldn't stop with me.'

'What 'er done with Hopsy? Hopsy, Hopsy where you gone, you little varmint?' Ma Lovell said loudly. Miss Lee was playing *Hark the Herald Angels Sing* and the curtains opened.

Pattella sat by the manger looking at the baby Jesus lying in his bed of scarlet Christmas flowers, and Chris stood beside her. The shepherds came in and knelt down, and the hall was very quiet.

'Hopsy, Hopsy, where 'un got to?' said Ma Lovell.

'Hush,' said Mrs White.

Then the kings came in with their precious gifts, and then Hopsy came with them.

'Help,' whispered June.

'Leave 'un,' said Liberty, as Dusty tried to get Hopsy under the donkey's blanket, but Hopsy put his thumb in his mouth and scrambled on to Pattella's lap.

''Er's Hopsy,' said Ma Lovell. 'Hopsy, come 'ere, you little devil.' But Hopsy just sat on Pattella's knee and stared into the darkness of the hall. Suddenly Chris had an idea.

'Look, an angel has come to see baby Jesus,' he said.

'Lovely little angel, ain't 'ee?' said Pattella, rocking Hopsy in her arms though he didn't look much like an angel with a fruit gum dribbling down his chin.

Miss Lee began *Away in a Manger* very softly because Pattella was supposed to sing the first verse, but Pattella rocked Hopsy in her arms and began to sing the Gypsy lullaby instead. They'd asked her to sing it and now Ma was there and Hopsy, and Pattella sang the Romany song. She fixed her black eyes on the front row of the hall and sang in a small reedy voice. Miss Lee stopped playing, and Pattella started another verse. This time Ma Lovell sang too and Liberty looked up from his writing and pushed back his hat and sang as loud as he could. The Romany words echoed round the hall, and after that there was deep silence.

Then everybody clapped, and Pattella picked the Christmas flowers out of the manger and gave them to the Chairman of the Council with a nice curtsey. The Chairman of the Council patted her head and Chris jumped down.

'Mary's a Gypsy and the Gypsies got nowhere to stop,' he said breathlessly, but everyone from the front row was going towards the door. The Christmas play was over.

Ally Gives a Christmas Present

THELMA SANGSTER

There was a tingling feeling of excitement in the air at 33 Beckett Street. Christmas was coming.

Ally and Mum stirred the Christmas pudding. It smelt sweet and spicy. Andy stood by, ready to lick spoons.

Mum opened the kitchen cupboard. She brought down six little silver things from a high shelf. She washed them well and popped them into the pudding mix for the family to 'find' at Christmas dinner.

Ally's eyes sparkled as Mum stirred them in – wishbone, cradle, train, button, dog and sledge. She hoped she would find the cradle. Andy wanted the train.

There was a sound of hammering coming from the garden shed. Dad was making something – but they weren't allowed to see it.

'It's a doll's house,' Ally confided to Belinda May as she put the baby doll to sleep in her cradle. She tucked her in with the pretty patchwork quilt Mum had made. It was special – Mum had made it from little bits of material left over from making dresses for Ally.

'It's a car! Vroom... vroom,' shouted Andy, running into the room and out again.

Christmas was coming at play-group too. Miss Carter had taught the children to sing carols. They had decorated the hall with tinsel and streamers and stuck cotton wool on the windows and made a snowman out of white tissue-paper scraps stuck on a cone of newspaper.

'Everyone will have a part in the Christmas play,' Miss Carter had told them. First she chose the youngest children to be lambs. They wore woolly face-masks and tails, and crawled in, making bleating sounds.

Then Miss Carter picked Lindy to be Mary, and gave her a baby doll to hold. Ally frowned. Lindy always got the nice parts.

Gary was to be Joseph. He had to lead Mary in and say, 'Innkeeper, my wife is tired. Have you any room in the inn?'

And Sandra (who giggled a lot) had to answer, 'No, there is no room in the inn, but there is room in the stable. Follow me.'

'Ally, you can be a shepherd,' Miss Carter said, handing her a striped curtain for her costume. Ally made a face. She wanted to be Mary, and hold the baby Jesus.

Andy could speak up in a nice loud voice, so Miss Carter made him the Angel. But Andy was against the idea.

'Want to be a racing-driver,' he announced. And he vroom-vroomed to the end of the hall.

Miss Carter fetched him back. 'Well, we can't have a racing-driver in this play. You'll have to be an Angel,' she said in a voice that meant, 'It's fixed.'

But somehow rehearsals had not gone at all smoothly.

Ally had to point to the Angel and say, 'What's that light?' But she was never ready, and had to be poked.

The Angel was supposed to say, 'Behold I bring good news. A Saviour is born today' . . . but he kept forgetting his words.

And when Gary said to Sandra 'Idd-keeper, by wife is tired. Have you eddy roob?' (because he had a cold), Sandra had a fit of giggles and spoilt her lines.

But Miss Carter was very patient. 'It will be all right on the day when your parents come,' she said.

So today Mum was making the Angel a long white robe out of an old sheet. Andy tried it on. When he lifted his arms the wings spread out.

'Vroom-vroom,' shouted Andy, jumping off the sofa. He tripped on the hem and made a crash landing. His yells brought everyone running.

Dad picked him up. 'Come and see what I've been making,' he said.

They all went out to the shed. It was growing dark in the garden, but the first star of the evening hung in the clear, frosty sky. It winked at Ally.

In the bare wooden hut Dad had hung up a storm lantern. Its light shone on a group of small figures on the work-bench. They were carved from wood, with painted faces and bodies. Three had gold crowns on their heads. There were shepherds and some animals too.

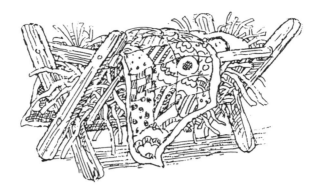

Ally could see Mary dressed in blue by the manger, with Joseph standing beside her. The little baby in the crib looked like a real baby, asleep. She though he looked cold.

'Ooh... lovely,' said Ally. 'Can we keep it?'

'No, I've made it for the shop window display to remind people what Christmas is all about,' said Dad. 'It's to remind them that the reason we give presents is because God gave his Son for us.'

Ally glanced round the bare cold shed. She looked at Dad's tools all neatly laid out. She smelt the wood shavings, swept into a neat pile. Her guinea-pigs Spick and Span squeaked softly from their winter quarters on a nearby shelf.

Ally turned and ran from the shed, up to her bedroom. Snatching up Belinda May's soft warm quilt of patchwork squares she said to the little doll, 'Jesus needs it, Belinda May.' She put the doll into her own bed and Belinda's eyes closed trustingly in sleep.

Out in the shed Ally placed the patchwork quilt over the little figure in the cradle. 'A present for baby Jesus,' she said.

Mum put an arm around her. Ally glimpsed the star, winking in the cold night, through the shed window. She suddenly felt all right about being a shepherd in the Christmas play.

Going over to the guinea-pigs she took Spick and Span from their nesting-boxes. Then she bent over the cradle, holding one under each arm. 'Look – sheep,' she said.

Suddenly the Angel spoke up loud and clear: 'Behold I bring you good news. A Saviour is born today...' And he lifted his arms to let the wings show.

And Ally knew everything was going to be all right.

King for a Day

RUTH NEWMAN

'You can be a king,' said Miss Jones to Mark. A king? Mark wasn't too sure about that. Miss Jones had been telling them a story about a baby, born long ago. The afternoon was hot and he'd almost been asleep. He couldn't understand what a king was doing in a story about babies. And this baby was born in a stable.

'Funny,' thought Mark, 'my little brother was born in hospital.' Also, this baby had slept in a cow shed in a manger with lots of straw.

'Ugh!' thought Mark. He knew all about smelly cows. His uncle John lived on a farm. Straw too! How prickly it must have felt. His baby, Christopher, had a nice warm carry cot with a blue blanket. He slept in a warm bedroom in their house.

Then Miss Jones had said that some kings had come to see this baby. The vicar had called to see his baby. A nurse came to see the baby a few times. But so far the Queen hadn't been.

Miss Jones said, 'Mark, you can be the king who took gold to the baby.' Fancy taking gold to a baby. Perhaps it could have been used to buy a proper bed! His friends, Peter and Richard, were being kings too. They had to carry some funny presents. Fr... fran... frankincense and mum... mum... myrrh... he found it hard to say the names. Well, Christopher had been given some strange presents, a silver goblet for one.

Miss Jones said that the frankincense and myrrh were special perfumes used in church. Mark's mum seemed to use a lot of smelly things when she bathed Christopher. But what use would frankincense and myrrh be to a baby?

Later that week Miss Jones told them more about the baby. Mary and Joseph, the baby's mum and dad, had gone to Bethlehem for a special ceremony. Mary rode on a donkey. When they arrived they had nowhere to stay. Bethlehem was crowded and that's why they had to stay in a stable. When the baby was born they gave him the name Jesus.

'No argument,' said Joseph. 'He's to be called Jesus.' Phew, the arguments there had been between Mark's mum and dad over what to call his new baby.

'But what about the kings?' Mark asked Miss Jones.

'Oh, they came from far lands, riding on camels. There were three of them, wise and clever men. They met up on their journey because they were all following a STAR. The star had moved across the sky until it seemed to shine over Bethlehem. The wise kings were looking for a baby,' said Miss Jones.

'Who would expect to find a baby in a stable?' thought Mark.

Soon all the class were involved in preparations for the Christmas play. They learnt new songs and where to stand. Jenny, who was Mary, and Paul, who was Joseph, had to practise walking to the stable. Paul didn't like putting his arm round Jenny. The practices in the hall began to get a little boring.

Miss Jones found some sort of cradle. Not much like Uncle John's cow feeder, but still, it did have straw in it.

One day Miss Jones took all the costumes out of a big chest. They smelled a bit funny. Mark, Peter and Richard all had long robes and crowns. It was tricky walking in them. Mark felt quite different when he put on his costume. Paul didn't seem to mind walking with Jenny either once they were dressed up. Mark was given a box covered in gold foil to carry and Peter and Richard were given strange looking jars.

At home, Mark practised walking up and down the hall dressed in his mum's dressing gown and a paper crown he'd made. He felt proud dressed up, like a real king.

The night before the big day Mark helped to bath his baby brother. Mum let Mark nurse him for a little while. Christopher felt warm to hold and he smelled nice, he cuddled up to Mark and even tried to smile at him.

'Tell me about baby Jesus, Mum. Why was he so special that kings visited him?'

'Yes, he was special,' said Mum. 'He must have been or those rich, proud and clever men would never have travelled so far to see him. They believed that one day he would be a king.'

'And was he?' asked Mark.

'No, not a king like they were kings. But when he grew up he was extra kind and loving and he wanted people everywhere to be the same. So, just as Jesus did, we try to love and care for one another.

'Just like we love and care for baby Christopher?' whispered Mark.

'Yes, just like that,' said his mother.

The big day arrived at last. Gran came with his mum to watch. Mark felt funny inside. The hall was packed.

Most of the children were sitting at the front of the hall. They were going to sing the carols. The ones who were dressed up were waiting in the classroom for their turn. The angels looked pretty.

'Pretty silly!' said Richard.

'Quiet!' said Miss Jones.

Mary and Joseph walked slowly down the hall in the gap between the rows of chairs. The children sang about a little donkey.

'I'm sure my Uncle would have found us a real donkey,' said Mark.

'Not now, Mark!' whispered Miss Jones.

'Or even a real sheep for the shepherds.'

'Quiet!' said Miss Jones again.

'What about a camel for us?' asked Peter.

'Don't be silly, Peter, quick it's your turn after this song.'

Suddenly, they were all three walking into the hall. Everyone was singing about kings riding to Bethlehem. Mark felt very nervous. He could tell Richard was wanting to giggle and Peter looked as if he were going to be sick.

Before the song had finished they had reached the stable. Mark no longer felt nervous. He laid down his gift beside the cradle and bowed low. Peter and Richard did the same. Then everyone sang a happy song.

Mark felt happy and pleased, glad and proud. He was sure that if he had seen the real baby Jesus he would have wanted to give him a real present – not a cardboard box wrapped in gold foil. He closed his eyes and imagined he really was a king, really there at the stable, and he knew he would have loved Jesus.

Nativity Play Plan

JAMES BERRY

Leader: Sistas and broddas and everybody,
same like we did sey –
we a-go keepup Jesus birtday.

Members: Yes! Yes!
We a-go keepup Jesus birtday.

Leader: Mista Daaswell, bring yu donkey
Mas Pinnty yu bring yu pony.
All will behave good-good with clappin and praisin.

Mista Slim, yu bring two sheep
wha will neither move nor sleep.
Faada B – two bright wing fowl
what will look like them nevva bawl.

Sistas and broddas and everybody,
we a-go keepup Jesus birtday.
We sey we a-go do that.
A wha we sey we a-go do?

Members: We a-go keepup Jesus birtday.
Yes! Yes!
We a-go keepup Jesus birtday.

Leader: Cousin Sue, bring yu big sow.
Aunt Cita, bring yu red cow.
All will behave good-good with singin and dancin.

Beagle and Man-Tom and Big Ben,
yu come turn in-a Wise Men.
Modda M will bring her new-new child
to be the new Jesus child.

Sistas and broddas and everybody,
we a-go keepup Jesus birtday.
We sey we a-go do that.
A wha we sey we a-go do?

Members: We a-go keepup Jesus birtday.
Yes! Yes!
We a-go keepup Jesus birtday...

Little Brown Jesus

JOAN O'DONOVAN

'Pause,' I said again. 'You forgot the pause.'

The Virgin Mary's eyes rolled in her brown-sugar face.

'Yes, miss,' she said resignedly.

'Try once more. And watch me.'...

'*Pause*!' I said.

This time, Heliotrope bared her teeth in a wide, semi-circular grin.

'You do have to keep saying it!' she told me with enthusiasm.

I gave up. It was the fifteenth time that morning.

'All right, that'll do for now.'

They were round me then, the children, twittering. This was the backward class, only at Gudge Street we called it 'Opportunity'. Gabrielle had torn his halo and the fifth shepherd lost his lines.

'You must remember to watch the beat,' I said to Heliotrope as I put a stitch in the halo. 'I'm not standing up there to scare the birds.'

Heliotrope jigged happily and her pencil-pigtails, each harvested from a square of black wool and tied with red tape, stood on end... all eight of them.

'In Jamaica we got things like a drain, miss, with holes; and the boys cover them with grass so the birds don't see, and when they stand there they catch their legs and the boys put them in cages.'

She giggled and flattened her nose with a gesture of splayed fingers.

'Crool thing!' shouted Jim...

The class took it up.

'I'n't that Heliotrope crool, miss?'

'That Heliotrope' was her usual designation.

It wasn't that the children didn't like her. You couldn't dislike her any more you could dislike a puppy. But, with one exception, they preferred to keep their distance; for Heliotrope wasn't just naughty, she was dynamite. Even Jim, who had in his time thrown

166

a bucket of worms at the needlework mistress and hit the caretaker with his own broom, tried to protect himself when she was around by sidling up to me and mumbling superstitiously, 'I'n'it awful, miss, when there's *trouble?'*

I knew what he meant. Anything might happen. There had never been a colour problem at Gudge Street before Heliotrope came, but she had started one on her first day by calling us dirty whites. She was nearly lynched.

Oddly enough, it was Doreen Bax, the quietest girl in the class, who had become Heliotrope's friend; and now, it seemed, the play was going to put paid to that, for... it was most unfortunate... Doreen had assumed she would be the Virgin. She was a pale, pretty girl with an oval face, soft curling hair and wide blue eyes. And she always had been the Virgin. When a doubt arose, her mother sent me a sharp note, with cuttings from the local paper and a tinted photograph. That settled it. I'm obstinate too. In my play she was an angel. She had been sulking for a fortnight.

The morning of the dress rehearsal came... we were to act the play for the school in the afternoon... and, to kick off, Gertie Pugh stole the blob of red glass from the teacosy worn by the first wise man under the impression that it was what she called a *jool*. We managed to coax it from her knicker leg, but it took time; and as, in snatching it, she had broken the pin, I had to stick it back on the teacosy with glue. Then Jim (seventh shepherd) had a fit of nerves and knocked Joseph down; and the innkeeper's wife turned up with a yellow crinoline, long black gloves and a Dolly Varden hat, which was her mother's interpretation of my request for an old sheet and a couple of safety pins; and she unnerved me further by going out to assembly in the hat and gloves. But worse than all that, far worse, was the crisis over the doll.

I had suggested that a bundle wrapped in a shawl was all that was needed for a stage baby, but the class wasn't having any. Even Jim, who sucked up to me in his calm spells, couldn't bring himself to let that pass.

'Anyone'd see it wasn't Jesus in them clothes,' he explained. 'Up our church they had a doll, miss. And strore.'

Jim was an overgrown, loose-meshed boy with poor co-ordination and thick hobnails. Sometimes he fell flat on his face. It was news to me that he ever went to church.

'Yes, miss!' The class was censorious. 'You gotter have a doll!'

167

So I chose Doreen to bring hers. It seemed to cheer her up.

'And strore,' Jim reminded me. 'It i'n't right without strore.'

'All right, Jim, if you can get any straw, you bring it.'

But I wasn't sorry when he turned up without it, for I had troubles enough. Certainly, Doreen brought her doll, a little cuddly doll – a black doll. But Heliotrope brought a doll too, a white doll; and Heliotrope's doll was three foot tall and very much a lady doll.

'I got Jesus, miss!' she said.

The class gazed rapt at the sequined ball dress and stiletto heels.

'It's bigger'n the one I seen up church,' Jim gloated. 'I'n'it like a film star?'

He was right on both counts.

Doreen clutched her doll to her, and her face went slowly scarlet. Foolishly, I tried persuasion.

'That's a beautiful doll, Heliotrope, but I think it's a bit big.'

'Big, miss?' Heliotrope went into a squeal of incredulous laughter. 'Big? This nothing! Why...'

'Besides,' I interrupted, 'Doreen has brought hers. I asked her to, you know. It was all arranged.'

Heliotrope affected astonishment.

'Do you mean that little doll?' Her voice was objective. 'That small one? I don't think that's good enough to be Jesus, miss, that *little* doll.'

I had never before heard Doreen raise her voice. I should have said she was incapable of it. But it came now in a screech of rage.

'Jesus wasn't a *lady*!'

Heliotrope turned on her. The gloves were off.

'Jesus could've been anything he liked!' she snapped. 'He could've been a mouse, or a lion... anything! It says so in the Bible.'

'Well, he was a baby in the *play*, Heliotrope Smith, so there!'

I expected the class to concede that, but, hypnotized, the children continued to stare at the film star and Heliotrope made the most of it. She narrowed her cat-eyes to dull, spiteful slits.

'Your doll's black!' she said baldly. 'The one thing Jesus never was was black. Jesus was real white.' She jutted a shoulder contemptuously. 'Little black thing!'

'Babies *are* little! We got one.'

'Little! Only bad, low-class babies are little! Why, I seen babies in Jamaica, *huge* babies! Their mammies could hardly lift them...'

'Babies are little,' Doreen repeated stubbornly. 'And my doll says "Ma-ma" like our baby does.'

Furious, she took the coloured doll and it bleated.

'So does mine! So does mine!'

Heliotrope tipped her doll at a dangerous angle. It had a powerful voice, like a tenor bull...

Doreen began to cry.

'Mine walks too!' she sobbed.

Heliotrope cast a triumphant eye round the class.

'Mine walks...' she screamed '...*and* wets!' And snatching up the ball dress, she revealed an incongruous pair or rubber pants.

It was time to stop the demonstrations. We would rehearse, I said firmly, with a bundle. The dolls were put aside and the decision shelved till the afternoon. With luck, one of the children might come out in a rash and have to be sent home.

At lunchtime, I took four more aspirins and went to lie down. The rest of the staff were in the canteen, so I had the staff-room to myself. The playground noises came filtered by the distance, rare and a little unearthly. I began to relax. The Head, after all, was a reasonable man. He wouldn't expect the Opportunity class to do more than lumber on and lumber off; and let's face it, I told myself, that's all they'll do. But did it matter? Whatever happened, the Opportunity class would be delighted. The Opportunity class had a great welcome for itself.

I was woken from a light doze by a pounding of boots on the stairs, and a terrible boy called Fisher burst in.

'You're wanted,' he told me.

He was wearing Edwardian dress, a long velvet drape and a tie no thicker than a shoelace. I had an impulse to ask him why he did it, but thought better of it.

'Who wants me?' I said instead. 'What is it?'

'A man wiv an 'orse and cart.'

It came to me like a symbol in a dream. I went downstairs, past the children swinging on the main door and out into the stale cold of Gudge Street. A woman walked by with a cabbage under her arm and a thick, worn purse in her thick, worn hand. Opposite, a youth lounged in a doorway eating chips from a bag. But there was no man that I could see, and no cart, no horse.

Kennick, on playground duty, wandered across.

'You owe me fifty pence.' He held out his hand. 'Walton couldn't find you. I sent Fisher, but the bloke wouldn't wait so I paid.'

'What for?'

'He said for obliging.'

I gave him the money and he looked at me curiously.

'Aren't you having fun!'

I didn't answer. I was thinking of my predecessors. One was still in hospital. I decided that I must be less sincere about my job. I must look after myself. I must keep a grip on reality; and next time I mustn't take so much aspirin.

But back in the classroom the nightmare met me, and it had nothing to do with mental balance. Straw. A mountain of straw. My desk was submerged, and the top of the radiator showed like the fluted edging of a flower bed. Spikes stuck at bizarre angles from the inkwells, and the air was thick with dust.

I stared stupidly round. I tried to wade forward, but barked my shin against the nature table which I could no longer see. I was rescuing the terrapins when Jim skated up.

'I ain't letcher down!' he told me happily. 'My dad says it's all right about the strore. The fifty pence was for the rag-and-bone man what lent him the 'orse. There was too much to go on his barrer.' He tossed a handful joyously. 'It's more than we had up our church.'

'It was very generous of your dad, Jim,' I said in a controlled voice.

'Tha'sall right, miss!' He threw another fistful up and it came down on me. He began to scratch. 'Fleas,' he said cheerfully. 'You don't half get a lotter fleas in strore.'

170

When Heliotrope came in I saw she had a long scratch on her cheek, and Doreen had the beginnings of a black eye. The class was exhausted. It must have been quite an emotional dinner hour.

But there was still fight in Heliotrope.

'Miss,' she demanded in the voice of one who will be trifled with no longer, 'which doll is Jesus?'

She didn't press her point, but I knew that look. If I wasn't careful, I could whistle for my Virgin.

Weakly, I glanced at Doreen. The swollen eye gave her an air of unwonted toughness, and for the first time I detected a resemblance to her mother. I felt I couldn't stand that either; so I asked myself the question that I had the occasion to ask myself many times with the Opportunity class: What would King Solomon the wise have done now?

And then it came to me, the one solution possible.

'We're going to have two Jesuses,' I said crisply.

Now that's where I hand it to an Opportunity class. There's no conventional prejudice.

'Smashing!' shouted Jim. 'They only had one up our church!'

Heliotrope brightened. She began to giggle. Doreen's face lit into a slow, satisfied smile. They looked at each other. Heliotrope pranced up and flung an arm round her rival's neck.

'You know,' she said judicially, 'mebbe your little Jesus isn't so black as I thought. Mebbe he's just a little brown Jesus.'

She took him up and began to nurse him.

So the film star lay in the crib; or half of her did. The nylon legs and stiletto heels were embedded in the merciful strore.

And, really, it was astonishing, but no one forgot his words, not even Jim. True, the jool came unstuck and fell at Mary's feet, but I liked the symbolism; and, when it came to it, Doreen looked interesting in profile, and I alone could see the ripening eye. As for Heliotrope, she rooted the Christmas story in Gudge Street, and Gudge Street paid her the tribute of absorbed silence. After all, these were the threatened children, the children of flits, evictions and eight to a room: they understood about having it the hard way.

I watched from the wings as the play swept through to its climax. There was just the solo now, and it would be over for another year. I raised a hand, the other on the pulley; and Heliotrope, alone on the stage, waited as I had told her to wait. The air was so still that I heard a man whistling a street away.

171

But when we had both counted to ten, she looked, not at me but at the bundle in her arms; and instead of beginning 'Away in a Manger', she sang to a beat that I recognized as calypso:

'Little brown Jesus, go sleep um don't cry...'

I turned frightened eyes to the school. There was a sense of feet tapping, but not a foot moved: and Heliotrope, easing herself as a mother nursing a baby might, sang with a sort of loving exasperation:

> *Little brown Jesus, go sleep um don't cry;*
> *When you cry so bad you make Mammy boil.*
> *Your Daddy Joseph he gone saw wood,*
> *And Lord God he is busy with the weather,*
> *So you go sleep, you brown-skin boy,*
> *Your Mammie done smack you when you don't go sleep...*

The voice got quieter. Heliotrope cast me a single authoritative glance, and the glance said *Curtain!*

'Um Lord... U-u-um Lor-ord!'

I let the curtain slowly down.

Silence continued for perhaps five seconds; then thunder broke. I dashed on to the stage and caught Heliotrope up. She giggled wildly, and flung her arms and legs round me like a monkey.

'What you crying for, miss?'

'Write it out! You must write it down for me, that song! Do you hear?'

I felt the heart go out of her.

'Yes, miss,' she said dully.

I remembered then. For Heliotrope, writing was a punishment and a pain.

'No, no, silly!' I said. 'I like your song. I want to have it! You tell me the words: I'll write them down myself!'

She threw herself back and squealed with laughter, her limbs twitching with diabolical energy again.

'Hoo! I thought you was cross!' She looked at me now as if she feared I was daft instead. 'I just sing to brown Jesus, see, miss? Any old words. They just come.' She giggled again. 'I forgot to watch for you scaring them birds didn't I?'

8

Donkey Tales

A section of donkey tales was not part of the plan for this book, but somehow the donkey refused to be left out. In the land where Jesus was born there are donkeys everywhere, even today – donkeys carrying heavy loads, donkeys carrying heavy people. So surely a donkey must have made that journey with Joseph and Mary, from Nazareth to Bethlehem.

What the Donkey Saw

U. A. FANTHORPE

No room in the inn, of course,
And not that much in the stable,
What with the shepherds, Magi, Mary,
Joseph, the heavenly host –
Not to mention the baby
Using our manger as a cot.
You couldn't have squeezed another cherub in
For love or money.

Still, in spite of the overcrowding,
I did my best to make them feel wanted.
I could see that the baby and I
Would be going places together.

The Christmas Donkey

GILLIAN McCLURE

There was once a donkey dealer who had three donkeys. Two of them, Ebed and Obed, were gentle, obedient creatures. The third, Arod, made trouble whenever he could.

'Too wild and proud,' the donkey dealer would often mutter.

One day, when the donkey dealer was in the stable grooming Ebed and Obed, news came that all the people in the land had to return to the town of their birth to pay their taxes.

'And how will they travel?' the dealer asked himself happily. 'By donkey, of course. Everyone will need donkeys. With the money I'll get for these three, I can buy six more. There'll be no end to it.'

At that moment, Arod came into the stable, upset the water bucket with his head, and kicked it against the wall.

'And you'll be the first to go,' the man shouted at him.

The first traveller to arrive was a rich baker, and the dealer wasted no time in showing him Arod.

'You won't regret it if you take this one,' he said. 'He's keen-eyed and sure-footed.'

But the baker saw the wildness in Arod's eyes and thought differently.

'No, not that one,' he said. 'But I'll pay you in gold for this one,' he added, pointing to Ebed. So the deal was done. As the baker left, Arod stole a loaf from his bag.

'A richer man than you will choose me,' he brayed angrily. 'Only a king is good enough for me.'

The next to arrive was a wealthy wine-merchant. Again the dealer pointed to Arod.

'This is the animal for you,' he said. 'Keen-eyed and sure-footed.' But Arod kicked out his hind leg.

'No, not that one,' said the merchant firmly. 'But I'll pay you in silver for this one.' And he took hold of Obed's bridle.

Arod tore the wine merchant's robe with his strong teeth.

'Just wait,' he snorted. 'My king will come, a finer man than you'll ever be.'

A little later, a poor carpenter arrived. His wife, Mary, was going to have a baby soon and he needed a donkey to carry her to Bethlehem.

'You're lucky,' said the dealer. 'I have one donkey left and he is my best: keen-eyed and sure-footed, gentle and brave.'

Joseph hesitated. 'I don't have much money...' he began.

'He's yours,' said the donkey dealer hurriedly. But Arod had other ideas. This man was no king. Arod wanted to run, but there in the doorway stood Mary. Arod bowed his head and waited quietly while she climbed on his back.

The donkey dealer watched them go. 'The others will arrive safely,' he thought, 'but I'm afraid Arod will give those two nothing but trouble.'

For a while Arod trudged along the stony road; then his patience began to run out. He spotted a patch of thistles and lunged towards them, determined to roll in them and shake off his heavy burden. Suddenly he heard a strange roaring in his ears and stopped short.

Joseph came running up. 'You are indeed brave,' he said. 'I didn't see that lion blocking the path. You have saved our lives.'

Mary stroked Arod's neck gently, and as they set off once more, his load seemed lighter.

On and on they travelled. Arod grew tired and, as night fell, he spotted some wild goats grazing in a meadow and decided to join them. But a falling star flashed across the sky, startling him, and he reared up sharply.

'Oh, donkey,' said Joseph. 'I failed to see the snake, curled in the shadows. But, thanks to your sharp eyes, we can go safely on our way.'

Arod was pleased, and as Mary patted him lovingly, the stars shone brighter.

The next day, their route took them down into deep valleys. Arod hated it. He jerked his head away from Joseph and was about to bolt when a shining figure appeared before him. Joseph caught Arod's reins.

'You are as sure-footed as we were told,' he said gratefully. 'We would certainly have fallen into that ravine.'

Mary caressed the donkey's velvety ears. Arod walked on. The path was less stony and his burden much lighter now.

At last Joseph, Mary and Arod reached a hill above Bethlehem. As they watched a stream of travellers passing through the gates, Joseph said sadly to Mary, 'It will be hard to find a room for you to rest in tonight.'

But Arod was untroubled. He trotted calmly on, carrying Mary proudly through the gates.

At the first inn they visited, the innkeeper just laughed. 'You're far too late,' he said, guffawing. 'The whole world got here before you.'

Arod, meanwhile, had gone to the stable at the back of the inn. There he met Ebed, smugly chewing a mouthful of hay.

'You'll never find a room in Bethlehem,' Ebed said. 'You must have dawdled. I brought my rich baker straight here and he's comfortably settled.'

Arod snorted. 'I carried something more precious than any baker,' he said.

At the second inn, Joseph fared no better.

'Be off with you,' shouted the innkeeper. 'Can't you see we're full?'

At the back of this inn Arod found Obed, looking pleased with himself.

'You must have lost your way,' Obed said. 'The town's full up, you know. My wine merchant was very content with the smooth, swift ride I gave him.'

'My charge was worth a hundred wine merchants and all their wine,' retorted Arod.

At the third inn, the innkeeper's wife took pity on Mary.

'You won't find a room anywhere,' she said. 'But we can give you stable space, if you like. It's warm and dry.'

So Arod led Mary and Joseph to the stable. He told the ox, the sheep, and the hens to make room for Mary, who lay down on the straw. A strange light filled the darkness and the air was still.

Then they heard a cry – the cry of a newborn baby. The animals moved closer and knelt before Mary, Joseph, and the baby.

'Lay him in my manger,' lowed the ox.

'Cover him with our hay,' bleated the sheep.

'Our feathers will make a soft pillow,' clucked the hens.

There was no room for Arod to kneel with the others, so he nipped the ox on the rump. The ox jumped, the sheep baaed, the hens flew up to the rafters, and Arod knelt down before his king.

'Thank you for choosing me,' he brayed softly.

The baby smiled.

The Donkey's Christmas

ANON

Plodding on,
From inn to inn,
No room to spare,
No room but a stable bare.
We rest,
And the following morning Jesus is born.
I gaze on the wondrous sight.
The King is born,
The King in a stable.
I see great lights,
Lights that are angels.
Everyone comes to see this sight.
I carried Mary,
Holy Mary,
Last night.

The Naughty Donkey

AGATHA CHRISTIE MALLOWAN

Once upon a time there was a very naughty little donkey. He *liked* being naughty. When anything was put on his back he kicked it off, and he ran after people trying to bite them. His master couldn't do anything with him, so he sold him to another master, and that master couldn't do anything with him and also sold him, and finally he was sold for a few pence to a dreadful old man who bought old worn-out donkeys and killed them by overwork and ill-treatment. But the naughty donkey chased the old man and bit him, and then ran away kicking up his heels. He didn't mean to be caught again so he joined a caravan that was going along the road.

'Nobody will know who I belong to in all this crowd,' thought the donkey.

These people were all going up to the city of Bethlehem, and when they got there they went into a big *Khan* full of people and animals.

The little donkey slipped into a nice cool stable where there was an ox and a camel. The camel was very haughty, like all camels, because camels think that they alone know the hundredth and secret name of God. He was too proud to speak to the donkey. So the donkey began to boast. He loved boasting.

'I am a very unusual donkey,' he said, 'I have foresight *and* hindsight.'

'What is that?' said the ox.

'Like my forelegs – in front of me – and my hind legs – behind me. Why, my great great, thirty-seventh time great grandmother belonged to the Prophet Balaam, and saw with her own eyes the Angel of the Lord!'

But the ox went on chewing and the camel remained proud.

Then a man and a woman came in, and there was a lot of fuss, but the donkey soon found out that there was nothing to fuss about, only a woman going to have a baby which happens every day. And after the baby was born some shepherds came and made

180

a fuss of the baby – but shepherds are very simple folk.

But then some men in long rich robes came.

'V.I.P.s,' hissed the camel.

'What's that?' asked the donkey.

'Very Important People,' said the camel, 'bringing gifts.'

The donkey thought the gifts might be something good to eat, so when it was dark he began nosing around. But the first gift was yellow and hard, with no taste, the second made the donkey sneeze and when he licked the third, the taste was nasty and bitter.

'What stupid gifts,' said the donkey, disappointed. But as he stood there by the manger, the baby stretched out his little hand and caught hold of the donkey's ear, clutching it tight as very young babies will.

And then a very odd thing happened. The donkey didn't want to be naughty any more. For the first time in his life he wanted to be good. And *he* wanted to give the baby a gift – but he hadn't anything to give. The baby seemed to like his ear, but the ear was part of *him* – and then another strange idea came to him. Perhaps he could give the baby *himself* . . .

It was not very long after that that Joseph came in with a tall stranger. The stranger was speaking urgently to Joseph, and as the donkey stared at them he could hardly believe his eyes!

The stranger seemed to dissolve and in his place stood an Angel of the Lord, a golden figure with wings. But after a moment the Angel changed back again into a mere man.

'Dear dear, I'm seeing things,' said the donkey to himself. 'It must be all that fodder I ate.'

Joseph spoke to Mary.

'We must take the child and flee. There is no time to be lost.' His eyes fell on the donkey. 'We will take this donkey here, and leave money for his owner whoever he may be. In that way no time will be lost.'

So they went out on the road from Bethlehem. But as they came to a narrow place, the Angel of the Lord appeared with a flaming sword, and the donkey turned aside and began to climb the hillside. Joseph tried to turn him back on to the road, but Mary said:

'Let him be. Remember the Prophet Balaam.'

And just as they got to the shelter of some olive trees, the soldiers of King Herod came clattering down the road with drawn swords.

'Just like my great grandmother,' said the donkey, very pleased with himself. 'I wonder if I have foresight as well.'

He blinked his eyes – and he saw a dim picture – a donkey fallen into a pit and a man helping to pull it out... 'Why, it's my Master, grown up to be a man,' said the donkey. Then he saw another picture... the same man, riding on a donkey into a city... 'Of course,' said the donkey. 'He's going to be crowned King!'

But the Crown seemed to be, not Gold, but Thorns (the donkey loved thorns and thistles – but it seemed the wrong thing for a Crown) and there was a smell he knew and feared – the smell of blood; and there was something on a sponge, bitter like the myrrh he had tasted in the stable...

And the little donkey knew suddenly that he didn't want foresight any more. He just wanted to live for the day, to love his little Master and be loved by him, and to carry him and his mother safely to Egypt.

9
Loving and Giving

'God so loved the world that he gave his only Son… that through him the world might be saved.'
Christmas, the celebration of the birth of Jesus – is all about loving and giving. And that is the focus of the stories I have chosen for this closing section.

Getting Ready for Christmas

From *Happy Christmas, Little Angel*

RACHEL ANDERSON

Christmas is coming, but Gabrielle is not well. What she needs is friends to talk to. What she needs is presents. What she gets instead is the Potter family, with their weird ideas.

In the Potters' back garden, with the sun shining boldly over their vegetable plot and yellow dandelions blooming brightly in a crack in the path, while overhead the sky was blue without a cloud, it seemed almost like high summer.

Gabrielle pulled off her muffler, pom-pom hat, anorak and the top two jerseys. The youngest Potter was sitting up in its pram, dribbling and gurgling. Gabrielle tried not to look at it. The two eldest Potters were busily digging up potatoes. Don waved cheerily.

'Hi, Gabrielle!' he called. *'Felices Fiestas!'*

Gabrielle didn't understand what he meant so she took no notice and hurried stiffly past. The big brothers were always scary.

Inside the shed it was gloomy and dark. On the work-bench there were some jam jars of poster paint in various shades of reddish brown, some bits of cut-up newspaper in odd shapes, and a saucepanful of something a bit like dirty custard bubbling away on a camping stove.

Charity gave it a stir. 'Vegetarian glue,' she explained. 'No boiled horses' hooves here, just flour and water. Here, you can do some too if you like.' She handed Gabrielle a glue brush. The handle was sticky, and the brush part at the other end had only a few bristles left.

'Do some what?'

'Some getting ready, of course.'

'What for?' said Gabrielle.

'What d'you *think*, stupid?' said Benjy looking up from where he was crouched on the floor. He was the second youngest Potter. 'I wouldn't be painting a Christmas tree would I, if I was getting

184

ready for Bonfire Night?' His picture was of something brownish that looked a bit like a wet bush. His elbows were smudged with reddish-brown paint which dribbled down towards his wrists and splodged on to the card. Gabrielle was glad that at least she knew how to hold a paintbrush properly.

'That's just silly,' she said. 'It's not time. It's nowhere even near winter yet. It won't be Christmas for weeks and weeks. My mother told me.'

'She probably only said that to keep you from nagging,' said Charity.

Gabrielle realized that this just might be true. 'Anyway, I don't see what there is to get ready about.'

Once you'd decided what you wanted, and changed your mind a few times, then thought of a few more extra things to add to the list, there wasn't anything to do except wait and make sure you got them.

'There's all the things to make. Like the cards for a start,' said Faith. 'Benjy's in charge of those.'

Gabrielle looked down at Benjy's picture of a murky bush. He'd just finished painting HOpy CIRSMeSS across the top.

'He's spelled it wrong,' Gabrielle said.

'That's the way *I* spell it,' said Benjy.

'But it's not the normal way,' said Gabrielle. 'No one will know what you mean.'

'I don't want the normal way. I want my cards to be different. I'm sending hundreds and hundreds, for every friend I've got.'

Gabrielle wondered how someone as young as Benjy who hadn't even started school yet, could have got hundreds of friends already. She, who was much older, could only think of three – her two parents, and her rabbit. Four, if she counted Mrs Gale.

'The truthful fact is,' said Faith, who was carefully cutting out six-sided star shapes from newspaper, 'that if you count it in seconds, Christmas is indeed a long way off: four million, two hundred and thirty-three thousand and six hundred seconds away. However, actually it's only a mere seventy thousand, five hundred and sixty *minutes*, which, in simple terms for simple minds, is just seven weeks. And you'd be amazed how quickly weeks can fly by. So anybody who hasn't started their countdown to Christmas by now is going to be in BIG trouble when the time comes. Aren't they, Benjy?'

Benjy nodded, and the blob of brownish paint on his chin turned into a streak that made him look as though he'd been wounded.

'Anyway,' said Charity as she rolled up her sleeves, tied back her hair with a piece of string and set to work, measuring and folding pieces of card, 'getting ready's usually the best part.'

'No, it's not,' said Gabrielle. 'Getting presents is the best part.' For it suddenly occurred to her that as soon as she reached home, she could change the title of her list from *Get-Well Presents List* to *Important Christmas Presents List*.

'Presents! Pooh. Once you've unwrapped them, they're just a big disappointment.'

'No, they aren't!' said Gabrielle. 'Last year I got a lovely electronic teddy bear. All pink and fluffy and it had eyes that rolled and it waved its paws and sang Jingle Bells.' Then she remembered that in fact she hadn't been able to see it roll its eyes, nor wave its paws, let alone sing because it had to have a special kind of battery that you could only get in America where Gabrielle's father had bought it and even though Gabrielle and her mother had been all round town they hadn't ever managed to find the right type of battery it needed.

Thinking about the pink electronic bear that still couldn't do anything, reminded Gabrielle of some of the other presents she'd had last year, and how, once she'd torn off the paper and looked at them, she'd had a sick feeling as though the whole world was going to end. And then she remembered how her parents wouldn't play with her because they were too busy getting ready for their Christmas Night dinner party.

'Giving's better than getting anyhow,' said Faith. 'That's what it said in this magazine I read. You have to give and give until your heart breaks.'

'Not till it breaks,' said Charity. 'Just till it explodes with joy.'

'That's disgusting,' said Gabrielle, but then she remembered how, when she took her rabbit out its present, she'd felt happy and friendly inside even though the rabbit had seemed quite un-interested.

'Rabbits don't have Christmas.'

Benjy started on his second painting of a reddish brown bush, this time with HAPY CRHSTMS along the top.

Gabrielle didn't bother to tell him how to spell it properly.

Instead she said, 'If that's supposed to be a Christmas tree it's the wrong colour. I never saw a brown one.'

'It's not brown. It's meant to be red,' said Benjy. 'It just didn't mix very well.'

Faith said, 'It's not his fault. Charity mixed the powder all wrong. And now we haven't got anything left except brown and yellow.'

'I thought only little babies at playgroups made cards. At our house,' said Gabrielle, 'we buy proper ones, with gold on them.'

'Ooh yes, gold!' said Benjy. 'That'd be good. Better than silly milk tops that won't stick. I wish I had some golden paint!'

'And at our house, my mother and father have our address properly printed inside in gold letters so people know who they're from.'

'Wouldn't it be easier for your parents just to *write* their names in it with a pen?' said Faith.

'No, I think that gold sounds really nice,' said Benjy.

'And when the cards are finished, providing Benjy doesn't take *too* long,' Charity went on, 'there's the present holders to make.'

'Present holders?' said Gabrielle. 'What on earth are they?'

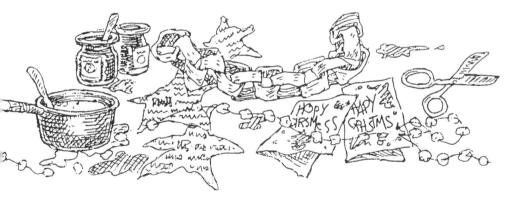

'And then the paper-chains. And the Christmas banner. And the front-door decorations. And the back-door decorations. And the bathroom decorations. And when we've done all them, we've got to design the thankyou letters so we'll be well ahead after Christmas is over. And then the wrapping paper. We haven't even started on that yet.'

'You can't *make* wrapping paper! You buy it in a gift shop,' said Gabrielle.

Charity ignored her, just as she'd ignored Benjy's request for gold. 'We're going to try potato-cut printing. When Don's finished digging for Mum's soup, he says he'll get us a few good big ones for our printing. Are you *sure* you can't help us a little bit because otherwise we'll never be ready and you're really in the way just standing there.'

The glue brush Charity offered Gabrielle was even stickier than before, while the jars of paint had all messed up into the same earthy colour.

'No, I'm still much too weak,' said Gabrielle. 'I nearly fainted this morning from Outback flu.'

Benjy looked up from his third Christmas card picture of a brownish bush. 'You look all right to me. And it's not Outback. How could it be? There's no germs in the Outback. It's all sand and sterile desert there. Nothing can grow. It's called *Vostok* flu, because it comes from Vostok, in Russia, which is the coldest place on earth.'

'Stop wasting time,' said Charity. 'You haven't even started on the paper-chains, have you?'

'I'm only telling old sick-bag here about flu,' said Benjy. 'Because when people are ill, they like to tell each other and share the information.' He turned back to Gabrielle. 'It's in Siberia. I should know, I had it. I shivered and shivered for three days without stopping, just like a person would in the coldest place in the world.'

Gabrielle wondered how Benjy, who was so young that he couldn't even spell Christmas properly, managed to know so many things.

'I learn things from my brothers, don't I?' he said. 'That's what brothers are for. Do you know, my brother Don is teaching himself how to say Happy Christmas in every spoken language in the world. Isn't that brilliant? I expect you sometimes wish you had some really clever brothers, then you'd know things too.'

'No, I do not,' said Gabrielle. And she gathered up her mittens, muffler, three sweaters, and anorak from where she'd scattered them around the shed and along the path. When she picked up her woolly hat, she saw that the two red pom-poms on top had gone. It looked as though they'd been snipped off with a pair of rusty scissors.

'Really, this is too too sickening,' she muttered. It used to be one of her mother's favourite phrases. 'It's the last time I *ever* come here again.' And she stomped away across the garden.

'Hey, *Feliz Navidad*!' Don called to her across the vegetable plot.

'And a smelly rotten Christmas to you too!' Gabrielle hissed and she went and stood by the Potters' front door, waiting for it to be time for her mother to fetch her. While she waited, she re-planned the get-well presents list into a Christmas present list.

She wished she'd brought the toy catalogue to help her remember what she'd already chosen and what was still waiting to be chosen. Her new list seemed shorter than the first one, too short.

A card shot through the Potters' letterbox on to the Potters' hall floor addressed to The Occupant. Since she was a temporary occupant of the house, Gabrielle thought it was all right to pick it up and read it.

DOUBLE GLAZING? YOU NEED IT *NOW*

BEFORE ICY WINTER COMES

it said. Since the Potters kept all their windows and doors wide open, Gabrielle knew that double glazing wouldn't be much use to them. So she used the card for writing out a new list.

CD player,
camera,
playdoh mixer,
diamond watch,
portable telly,
ballgown,
scrambling bike,
some sweets (lots),
lots and lots of other things.

A Stocking for a Kitten

HELEN KAY

This is a true story. The little girl 'Tanya' is the author's mother.

All day Tanya's grandmother, Babushka, sat and knitted stockings.

'Could they be for me?' Tanya asked Mother hopefully, looking at her own bare pink toes.

'Ask Babushka,' Mother said, but Tanya hesitated. Sometimes Grandmother, who was very old, answered questions in a very strange way. So Tanya sat with her kitten wherever Grandmother sat – in the kitchen, or in the garden, or under a tree in the shade. Tanya watched Babushka's old hands work on the steel needles, as the black stockings grew longer... and longer... but still not too long for Tanya who was really quite small.

The kitten, Kitka, watched, too. The moment the ball rolled from Grandmother's lap, Kitka pounced. Tanya picked her up and held her tight. This was no time for kitten fun. Tanya was hoping, hoping. She wanted new stockings to wear at Christmas. Tanya had to know. She could keep quiet no longer. Aloud, though in a very small voice, she asked, 'Babushka, are these stockings for me?'

Babushka's face was all wrinkled and creased, but her eyes were brown and shining and twinkly. She answered in her own and quite different way, 'Oh, no, these are for the first one.'

Tanya knew they were for her oldest sister, Vera, who was born first. Vera was quite tall, nearly as tall as Mother, so the stockings took a long time to finish – almost all summer. Tanya had to wait until the sunflowers by the garden gate had grown even taller than Father. Then the stockings were finished and Vera wore them to church on Sunday.

Once again Babushka took out a ball of thread and began a new pair.

Soon, it was too cold to sit in the garden or under a tree and

190

Babushka sat beside the great wall stove, where it was warm. Tanya sat there as often as she could. Even when she helped Mother, Tanya kept a watch on Grandmother, and hoped. The new stockings were red and very beautiful. Perhaps *this* time they *were* for her?

Mother understood Tanya's glance. She gave her a hug and said, 'You may ask Babushka. She will tell you.'

Tanya's voice sounded even smaller now. 'Babushka, are these for me?' she asked.

'Oh, no, they are for the second one,' Grandmother answered as she went on knitting. Tanya could see the wrinkles crinkling around her eyes, though she could not see the twinkle.

Olga was born second. Olga was also anxious to have new stockings, since hers were badly torn. She tried to hurry Grandmother. 'You are *too slow*, Babushka,' she said. 'Hurry with my stockings or it will be Christmas.'

Grandmother stopped working. She put the almost-finished stockings aside and said, 'I will not knit for you, Olga, until you show patience. You are rude.'

Olga tossed her head as though she did not care, but Tanya could see from the way she blinked that she was holding back the tears. Yes, Olga was sorry she had been rude. She was even sorrier to have to wear old stockings and she pulled her wide skirt over the big patches.

Tanya sighed. Olga would not have new stockings for the holidays. It made Tanya sad for her second sister, but she could not help feeling that *now* perhaps Babushka would begin on her – Tanya's – stockings.

A white ball of thread rolled again and the needles clicked.

'Babushka?' Tanya began, but she did not finish. Babushka answered with a question, 'Who is older than you?'

'Volya, my brother,' Tanya said.

Fortunately, Volya was a boy, and he wore socks. The socks were finished quickly, but now the snow was on the ground and the holidays were very near.

Tanya could tell because Mother was baking and roasting and sewing and cleaning. Vera and Olga were helping her. Volya was with Father, and Tanya was busy watching Babushka. Soon, soon it would be Tanya's turn, she hoped. There was no one else. She, Tanya, was fourth.

Tanya would not hurry Grandmother. She would not make the same mistake as Olga. For there was Olga's unfinished pair, still in the basket, and Olga with patches on her knees.

Tanya wanted to say, 'Tell Babushka you are sorry, Olga, so you, too, will have stockings for Christmas,' but she did not know how. Perhaps Olga also wanted to say, 'I'm sorry,' and did not know how? Tanya worried as she sat beside Grandmother, near the big stove which warmed them both, while the sunlight flashed on the steel needles and the kitten slept at their feet.

'My old hands are getting cold,' Babushka said. 'Get some straw for the fire.'

Tanya picked up a handful of straw and opened the little door to the big stove. She stuffed its mouth full. Bright red tongues of flame warmed the room. Now Tanya did not have to ask Babushka to hurry. Babushka knitted faster... much faster... so fast the yellow ball rolled around the room without the kitten's help.

Suddenly Babushka turned to Tanya and asked, 'Does your kitten have a stocking?'

'Oh, no,' Tanya said. Such a strange question! She had never heard of a kitten with a stocking.

'Then knit one, or Kitka will be cold this winter,' Babushka said.

Tanya was puzzled. How could she knit a stocking for her kitten? She scratched Kitka's furry head. The kitten purred, but Tanya could not tell if Kitka wanted a stocking or not.

Babushka pulled Tanya onto her lap and taught her how to knit. Together, they cast on stitches from a red ball, and a little tube was formed on three needles while Tanya worked with a fourth. A stocking, just big enough to go over a kitten's paw, was shaped in this way.

'Babushka is tired of knitting,' said Vera when she saw them working together.

Tanya wondered what Vera meant. Olga stomped in out of the snow, her nose and hands red. 'When you finish that kitten stocking, then Babushka will not knit for you any more. You'll be able to do it,' she explained.

Volya was right behind her, crying, 'But kittens have four feet! You'll never finish!'

Tanya went right on knitting her kitten stocking and sitting beside Babushka, who sat beside the stove, knitting the long yellow stocking. And Tanya worried. Perhaps this new pair was *not* meant for her? Were they getting too long so that she, little Tanya, could not wear them? Perhaps I will grow? Tanya thought, as she worked slowly, one stitch at a time. Had she knitted enough to cover Kitka's paw?

Tanya tried it on and Kitka became entangled in the needles and the thread. Even so, Tanya could see she still had much to do.

Babushka said, 'Measure it on your finger. When it is longer than your finger, it will be long enough for the kitten.'

Olga laughed as she went by, jealous of Tanya sitting so close to Grandmother and warmed by the fire. 'It's lucky Kitka hasn't grown into a big cat, yet. A kitten stocking will go quickly,' she said. However, Olga was being good in other ways. She helped Mother whitewash the walls and decorate them with painted flowers. She helped Mother bake the Christmas cakes.

Olga said, 'I will do your work, too, Tanya, since you are so busy.'

Tanya could see that Olga was looking at Grandmother's knitting basket, sadly.

'Thank you,' Tanya said softly, sorry for Olga. Everyone would have new stockings for the holidays – Vera and Volya, the kitten and Tanya, too, she hoped, but not Olga.

'How tall are you, Tanya?' Babushka asked.

She measured the stockings against Tanya's legs. They fitted just right! At last, Tanya knew for sure. They were hers!

'Mother, look!' Tanya cried. She wanted to call Olga, too, but stopped. Olga was acting as though she were very busy and Tanya knew it was because Olga felt so sad.

Tanya kissed Babushka and hugged her. 'Goodness, you haven't time,' Babushka said. 'You must finish the stocking for the kitten.'

Tanya sat down and knitted faster and faster. Volya held up his dog, to tease. 'Tanya, make stockings for my dog!' he cried.

Olga said, 'No, not for his dog, for my doll. She needs them so badly.' But Tanya knew that Olga meant she wanted them for herself.

Babushka did not seem to hear. Her eyes were closed and her old hands were resting.

Volya left to help Father bring in straw for the floor and sheaves of wheat to decorate the room. Mother told Olga to help Vera set the table. Tanya continued to knit. She must finish the stocking for her kitten. Tomorrow was Christmas Eve.

Just then, Grandmother opened her eyes. She looked sharply at Tanya's knitting. 'It is time now to bind off the stitches,' she said.

Pulling Tanya onto her lap again, they knitted two stitches together, until there were no more. Now the little red tube lay in Tanya's hand. It was a real stocking for a kitten.

Tanya tried it on Kitka. It fitted – except, of course, that Kitka had four legs. What good is one stocking? Tanya thought. 'Now I must make three more,' she sighed.

Suddenly Grandmother stood up. She asked aloud, 'What does a kitten need a stocking for?'

She pulled the red tube off the black kitten's paw and, opening the little door to the big stove, threw it inside.

The little tube hit the red coals and huffed up with hot air. Wrapped in fire, it glowed. It made a little puff, then it grew white as the purest ash. Finally, it disappeared. Or perhaps Tanya could not see? Her eyes were so full of tears.

Babushka mumbled some soft words. What was she saying? Then she turned to Tanya and said loudly, 'Now you are a knitter.'

Tanya saw Babushka's eyes all twinkly and she knew Babushka wanted her to come and sit on her lap, but she could not. She would not. She looked around for Mother to ask her why, but Mother was not there. So Tanya ran to her bed, hid under the big pillows and cried. She did not care that tomorrow was Christmas Eve, nor that she had new stockings to wear. No, she would never wear Grandmother's stockings. She hated her. There would be two others without stockings at Christmas besides Olga – the kitten and Tanya.

The kitten jumped up and licked Tanya's salty cheeks. As Kitka came closer and closer and cuddled, Tanya grew warmer and warmer, until she had to push the kitten away.

Suddenly, Tanya understood. She sat up. 'But, of course! Kitka does not need stockings, with her warm furry coat all over – even on her legs. But Olga does!'

Tanya climbed out of bed. Everyone in the house had already gone to sleep. She tiptoed over to Babushka's basket and pulled out Olga's almost-finished stockings. Tanya worked. She worked on them until the rooster crowed. Then, Olga's stockings were finished. Tanya put them on Olga's bed and went to sleep. She was tired.

When morning came, a shriek awoke her.

It was Olga's voice, loud and happy! Olga was jumping up and down for joy. 'Babushka, Babushka,' she cried, 'I love you. Thank you for finishing the stockings.' And she kissed her on both cheeks.

Babushka turned to Tanya. 'That was a good blessing I gave the kitten stocking, wasn't it, Tanya?' she asked.

Puzzled, Olga looked at Grandmother, then she looked at Tanya. Babushka said, 'Thank you, my Tanya.' Tanya had to lower her eyes. Her face was almost as red as Olga's new stockings.

'*You* did it, Tanya!' Olga shouted, pulling her little sister by the hands and dancing around with her, around and around and around, until they both fell down, hugging each other.

Vera and Volya and his dog came running to see what the noise was all about. The kitten came scampering, too.

'Look what little Tanya did!' Babushka called to Father and Mother.

Tanya looked up at Babushka's face, all creased and crinkled, and saw the bright brown eyes that had such a twinkle.

Tanya was so proud. She felt herself grow big... bigger. She was sure she was nearly as tall as Olga, and was suddenly afraid her own stockings might be too small. Quickly, she pulled them on. They looked beautiful!

And that is how they all had new stockings for the holidays – Vera and Volya and Olga and Tanya.

Not To Be Opened Before December XXV

NAN HUNT

The last week before Christmas was a disaster. Even Mum lost her cool and declared that 'Christmas plus kids equalled disaster'. Donna was the first to get into trouble when she ate all the coloured cherries out of the mixed fruit. I picked up the wrong can and sprayed deodorant instead of hair lacquer over Mum's head. Bennie hit one of the Christmas tree lights with a hammer 'to see what would happen'. Mum nearly raised sparks from him when she found none of the other lights would work. And Dad remarked that it looked like being a dull Christmas. 'And what's John been up to?' Dad asked then, looking at the rest of us with a jaundiced eye.

'He's been a positive angel!' Mum said. It was only in comparison, of course, but she should never have said it. It as good as said to John, 'Why don't you find something to get into?'

What he got into was a small, brown-paper-wrapped parcel in the back of Dad's desk, with a label marked: NOT TO BE OPENED BEFORE DECEMBER XXV. He shook it, felt it, smelt it. Nothing. No clues at all. John could read the label but he didn't dig the XXV bit, just thought it was kisses. There was no name on the label, but it looked important. He reasoned that as it *was* December, the parcel needed to be opened and the need grew and grew the more John thought, so he opened it.

Inside the paper was a box. Inside the box... well, it was bright and small but once the light got to it it began to grow and shoot out points of fire like cracker night sparklers. And it hissed in a gentle unfrightening way, growing brighter and brighter all the time and spitting more and more sparks until suddenly it flew out of the box and settled under the lampshade.

John had his face turned up and his mouth open and a couple of sparks landed on his eyes, making him blink. When he looked again, the light had gone and the box and paper were smouldering into black curls that floated into nothing when he stamped on them. The only part he salvaged was a corner of the label with XXV on it and that's the only reason I believed his story. He couldn't have written that himself.

That night our phone went crazy. First it was the police to warn Dad there had been a hold-up over at East Wilga and the bandits – a man and a woman – were thought to be hiding in Wilgagomungla Forest that came nearly up to our back yard. Then a city newspaper rang. Had we see the UFO that had been reported up our way?

'Hang on and I'll go and take a look,' Dad said. He came back in, picked up the phone and said, 'It's not a UFO, it's the Christmas star.'

John nodded his head in a satisfied way and whispered, 'Of course! That's what it is!'

Then all the neighbours rang. 'Hey, did you see the comet? It came shooting up from over your way, dragging this great tail of fizzing stars after it.'

'Couldn't have been a comet,' Dad said. 'They don't shoot up, they scoot along. Why does everyone else have all the fun? No, of course we haven't seen it.'

John went outside again and was gone for a long while. He came in at last and whispered to me, 'It's up there, you know.'

'What is?'

'The star.'

'You mean the comet?' I was always correcting John.

'Come and see.' So I went, and there it was, not shooting up or down or across, but just sitting right above our house, sparkling in the sky. 'Don't tell the others,' John said. 'I found it.'

'It's spooky,' I said, feeling goosepimples on my arms. 'But kinda nice, eh? And so bright.'

'It was in a box. I let it out. It just kept growing and growing and then it shot up in the air and sat under the lampshade and when I looked at it it dropped sparks in my eyes.'

'You're kidding!' But John shook his head and showed me the corner of the label.

On the news that night there was a lot about the UFO and why the Air Force wouldn't send fighter planes to investigate. There was even a bit about the bank hold-up at East Wilga and an accident on the highway between East Wilga and Harrisville. A truck driver had taken two people to the hospital, but when the police and ambulance arrived at the scene the other vehicles had disappeared.

'All we need now is for someone around here to knock off Santa's reindeer and we'll be in the news through to New Year,' Dad said. 'How about that, kids? No Santa Claus, eh?'

'It's OK,' Ben said. 'He's left all our presents already. I found...'

'Oh did you just!' Mum said quickly. 'Then you can stitch up your big mouth for once.' She looked warningly towards Donna, who still put out hay for the reindeer and a glass of cordial for Santa.

Donna said, 'Did you find the ones in the old dairy?' Mum and Dad looked like stunned mullets for a second or two but at that moment there was a crash outside, a strangled bellow from Agapanthus, the house cow, and a scream that made our hair stand on end.

We got jammed in the door trying to be first out, Dad grabbing the torch as he ran, and winning by superior weight. Agapanthus nearly knocked him flying as she headed towards West Wilga, muttering in cow language and dribbling long streamers from the cud. A battered old utility coughed to a stop in the middle of the driveway where Aggie had been resting, and out stepped the roundest lady I had ever seen in my life.

'Do you always leave your cows lying around so carelessly?' she said coldly to Dad. 'I hate to think what our meeting has done to our means of locomotion.'

'Don't worry about Agapanthus,' Dad said politely. 'She had full command of her legs, last I saw of her.'

'Lucky cow!' the lady said, and slid to a heap at Mum's feet.

'Quickly, into Aunt Kate's bedroom,' Mum said, and went on giving orders like a General so that each of us had something to do.

'Aunt Kate will go mad if anyone else sleeps in her bed,' Ben said. 'And she'll be here soon.'

'Let her!' Mum said. 'Gently now. That's it. Do you think you can walk if we help you?' The lady was game, though groggy. She held onto Dad and Mum and half walked, half slid up the path and into the house. Mum tucked her up in the sheets perfumed with dry lavender from the garden, and we all stood round and watched her drink tea.

'You're going to have a baby,' Donna said.

'However did you guess?' the lady laughed, patting the bulge under the sheet.

'Will you call her Donna after me?'

'It's a boy, Donna.'

'Then you can name him after us,' John said eagerly. He liked the idea of having a baby named after him.

'What are your names? David, Ben and John? I see. The trouble is, he's to be named Joshua because of his father...' and when she said 'his father' the lady began to cry and Mum shooed us all outside.

'I hope she lies light,' John said gloomily. 'There's three presents under that bed.'

Next morning Mum told us the lady had been part of the accident we'd heard about on the news. Her husband bumped his head, and once before when that happened he'd lost his memory and wandered about not knowing who or where he was. He'd wandered off this time and she'd gone into the forest looking for him, and the trail led towards our light. 'It blazed out so brightly, I kept heading for it.'

The trees in the forest were so thick Mum knew you couldn't see our light, and thought the lady might be a bit wandery herself. But John nodded his head and looked at me. 'The star!' he whispered.

'Comet,' I said automatically.

'You're in our Auntie's bed,' Donna told our visitor. 'Will you be our Auntie too?'

'OK. You can call me Auntie Polly.' She was nice and didn't mind us asking her things. Dad had gone off into the forest to look for her husband. She helped us decorate the Christmas tree and told us stories about when she was a little girl and what they did at Christmas. I think it took her mind off her lost husband.

Dad didn't come home that night and Mum rang the police. She called up all the neighbours too, and they organized a search party. Mum was scared the bank bandits might have him.

'Perhaps they'll cut off one of his ears and send it in an envelope with a ransom note,' Donna said, wide-eyed, and began to bawl.

Auntie Polly was very quiet for a while and then she gave a bit of a gasp and walked across to Mum and put her arms round her and told her not to worry. And she made us play hunt the thimble all round the house until we almost forgot about Dad. She was so anxious about her husband, but she didn't let on to us or act sorry for herself. John went outside every now and then to look up into the sky and he'd come in and nod to me.

'It's OK. It's still there. He'll come home for sure by the light of it.'

It was the morning of Christmas Eve and still Dad was not home. There were twenty men and a helicopter from the Search and Rescue Squad out looking for him and Auntie Polly's husband, and the bandits. Mum was trying to keep calm too but we could tell how she was feeling.

'What sort of Christmas will it be without Dad?' Ben said, looking sick.

'He'll come tonight with the shepherds,' John assured him, a fey look in his eyes.

'He'd do better to come with the Wise Men,' Ben said. '*They* brought presents.'

Donna was indignant. 'The shepherds brought a lamb. It says so in the carol. They couldn't help being too poor to bring anything else. I'd rather have a lamb than myrrh and that frank stuff.'

'What about a present for Aunt Polly?' I had to get Donna off that tack or she'd have been pestering Mum for a pet lamb, and Mum didn't need pestering just then. We talked about what we could do for Aunt Polly and finally decided to make her a hay pillow for the baby. Ben knew what to do, because he'd read about it in a craft book.

'All you have to do is bake the chaff to get all the wogs out of it, and then you stuff it in a pillow case and sew it up.'

Mum had to drive in to West Wilga to pick up Aunt Kate from the train. I knew she didn't want to leave us, but Auntie Polly persuaded her she was perfectly capable of looking after us. The house smelt heavenly of warm roast turkey and pudding boiled in a cloth and secrets wrapped up in pretty paper and excitement and worry and sadness and hope.

'Dad'll be home by Christmas for sure,' Mum said, 'so I'd better cook the dinner. It will be something to do.' She was a great believer in having everything done beforehand so we could enjoy Christmas together without spending too much time in the kitchen.

The sun went down in cloud and the night was dark and starless. When the dogs began kicking up a racket Ben said, 'That'll be Mum, now.' John slipped out of the back door to check on his star. And Auntie Polly, a little nervous about meeting Aunt Kate whose room she was in, said she felt like a bit of a walk. But Donna and Ben and I tumbled out onto the front verandah.

It wasn't Mum. It was the bank bandits. We walked right into their hands. They had Dad's four-wheel drive, but there was no sign of Dad and they weren't answering questions. They us go back into the house, and when they sniffed our Christmas dinner said they'd take that, thank you. And the man began stuffing things into a supermarket bag while the lady retired to the toilet. When the man grabbed the pudding, Donna gave a sort of moan, she loved pudding. And before you could say knife she'd stuck the broom handle between his legs and brought him crashing down. Ben and I sat on him and bent his arm back, but he'd hit his head when he fell and wasn't struggling. Donna looked scared but pleased. We didn't know till afterwards that John had set Bluey the cattle dog on guard outside the door of the toot and he wouldn't let the woman past. Then he'd hustled Auntie Polly away into the shed. When he came back he brought Dad's nylon rope and we tied it round and round the bandit till he looked like a half-undone Egyptian mummy.

In the middle of all this Mum and Aunt Kate turned up, expecting Dad to be inside because his vehicle was there. We all tried to tell them what had happened and Mum was trying to hide her worry about Dad, when she looked round and asked, 'Where's Polly?'

'In the shed, having her baby,' John said calmly. Well, fair dink, I'd never seen Mum and Aunt Kate move so fast. They just ran. And what with the woman yelling in the toot and Bluey growling and we kids all gabbling and a spat of rain on the roof, we didn't hear the search party arriving with Dad. Apart from a black eye and a sprained ankle, Dad was OK.

'It's pitch black outside,' one of the men said. 'We'd have been in trouble but for your big light. We could see it from everywhere.'

'The star,' John said.

'Comet,' I corrected.

What a night! The men had a cup of tea and took the bandits away to East Wilga and we were fussing round Dad when Mum came rushing in, flapping a towel and smiling all over her face. She just grabbed Dad and gave him such a hug and announced, 'It's a boy! And he's to be called Joshua Ben David, and they're both OK, and Aunt Kate is fixing her up!' Aunt Kate was a midwife.

'I told you Dad'd come with the shepherds,' John said. We were all so excited we put on our favourite carol record and turned up the volume, so that when the police arrived we didn't hear them, either, until they walked in. They were delighted to know the bandits were on their way to the lock-up but said they were looking for a pregnant lady. John got all funny, then, and told them there were no ladies in the house except Mum and Aunt Kate and Donna.

'You go tell Herod to jump in the lake!' he ended fiercely. 'He's not getting hold of Joshua!'

'You've got it wrong, son,' the big sergeant said. 'We've got *Joshua*, and we're looking for the lady to tell her that her husband's OK.'

Well! By that time the women had Auntie Polly back in Aunt Kate's bed, and the baby lying on our straw pillow in a drawer out of the wardrobe. And we all crowded round the doorway while the cop told her big Joshua was safe. She looked tired and pale, but when she heard the news her eyes began to shine as if the star were inside her and all her Christmasses had come at once.

'He was heading for the light when we found him. We took him straight to hospital, but don't worry. He's OK, the doc says.'

Afterwards I asked John. 'Did you mind little Josh not having your name?'

He shook his head. 'I had the star,' he said softly. 'I was the first to see it. You can't have everything.'

King of Kings

SUSAN HILL

It was Christmas Eve. Mr Hegarty had been about all day. He liked
to be about. He liked Christmas Eve. Everybody talked to everybody else and there was a lot of bustle; people were cheerful. He'd
been about the market, among the stalls and barrows. Then, he
and Jacko had stood for a long time on the corner, just for the
pleasure of watching everything. He'd had his dinner out – pie and
chips – and his tea, with a mince pie 'on the house'. Lotta, who
kept the cafe, had said, 'because ees Christmas'.

But now it was late. Dark. Now, everything was closing down.
They were sweeping up around the barrows, sprigs of holly and
paper from the oranges and a few lost sprouts.

'Goodnight, then. Happy Christmas.'

Lamps out. Blinds up. Shutters down.

The main road was jammed. The trains went along the line, full
of everyone going home. So Mr Hegarty and Jacko went home too.
Across the building site. Quiet now, the great crane still and silent.
It had a Christmas tree balanced on the very end, with lights and
decorations. But the men had finished at dinner time today.

Past the warehouses and wharves. Once, Mr Hegarty had been a
nightwatchman on the wharf. That was when the ships had
docked, years ago. There were no ships now.

Across the last bit of waste ground. Jacko's ears twitched.

Home.

Christmas Eve. The wind blew down alleyways, across the dark
wharves, smelling of rain and river. No snow. No star. But
Christmas Eve isn't often like the stories.

Mr Hegarty reached home. There was a carrier bag on the step,
with three wrapped-up presents inside, and a card. 'To Mr Hegarty
and Jacko and Cat, a Happy Christmas with love from Jo.'

Jo and his family lived next door. But they had gone away that
morning, to stay with his grandmother, for the holiday. One day,
they'd go away altogether. Everybody would. This was the last

street. Mr Hegarty didn't want to think about it.

Nothing inside the house had changed very much since he and Mrs Hegarty moved in, newly married; and since Mrs Hegarty died, nothing had changed at all. Mr Hegarty wanted it like that, just as it was and had always been and as she had left it.

He kept it clean and put things away in the same old places and polished the windows and blackened the hearth and washed up in the stone sink and slept in the big brass bed.

And every Christmas, he put up the decorations, around the pictures, and over the mirror and along the mantelpiece, with a wreath of holly on the front door, just as Mrs Hegarty always had.

It was very quiet. Mr Hegarty went into the scullery to wash his hands, then fed Jacko and Cat, put the kettle on, made up the fire, and sat beside it. And Mrs Hegarty sat beside him, smiling out from the silver photograph frame on the little table.

Later, the band came and played 'Silent Night' and 'Hark the Herald Angels', under the orange lamp at the end of the street, and the man with the collecting tin came down to Mr Hegarty's door and they had a chat. Then, they played one more carol, which was 'In the Bleak Mid-winter', because it had been Mrs Hegarty's favourite, before they went away. But for quite a while, the strains of trumpet and tuba and cornet, 'O little town of Bethlehem' and 'While shepherds watched' floated faintly back to him across the wharves and waste ground. Then, it was quiet again.

For the rest of the evening, while Jacko and Cat slept on the hearth rug, Mr Hegarty sat in his armchair, thinking, as people do, of other Christmases, good and bad and in between – but mostly good, for times past are golden in the memory to an old and lonely man.

At ten o'clock, he got up, and Jacko ran to the front door, and they went for their last walk, up the street and down again. There was nobody about, though some of the houses had lights on, glowing behind curtains, and two of them had Christmas trees in the windows.

And the wind still blew, down the alleyways and across the wharves and waste ground, with the smell of the river on its breath.

Christmas Eve. Mr Hegarty's heart lifted. It was still special, after all, there was no getting away from that.

Then, he let Cat out, locked up, wound his watch, and went upstairs to bed.

Some time after midnight, he woke again. At first, he didn't know why. There was no sound, except for Jacko, snoring softly. Then, there was something, a very faint, distant sound, not inside the house, out. Mr Hegarty put on his slippers, went downstairs, and opened the front door.

Everything was still. It had stopped raining and the wind had died down.

The moon shone.

Jacko came pattering down the stairs and stopped beside Mr Hegarty at the front door.

There it was again. Very faint. A mewling sound. Kittens?

Mr Hegarty put on his coat and shoes and took the torch. Then, he went out of the house and across the waste ground, towards the church. Jacko ran ahead, ears cocked, tail up.

There were railings round the old church, but the padlock on the gate was broken. The sound was louder. Mr Hegarty stopped. The moon came out again from behind a cloud. Jacko had trotted up the weed-covered path to the church porch and Mr Hegarty could see him standing beside something, wagging his tail. So he went too.

Here, the sound was loud and clear and unmistakable.

Mr Hegarty shone his torch.

On a ledge inside the dark, damp, cold stone porch of the church, stood a shallow cardboard box. Inside the box lay a baby.

It was very small, and wrapped in a scruffy piece of blanket.

'Now then!' said Mr Hegarty softly. 'Now then.'

But then he didn't know quite what to do.

He and Mrs Hegarty had never had any children. Mr Hegarty had never even held a baby. In his own home, there had been seven children, but as he had been the youngest, all the others had picked him up.

The moon went behind a cloud again, and the baby stopped crying and just lay. Jacko sat, waiting. 'Well,' said Mr Hegarty.

And then, because there was nothing else that he could do, he picked up the box with the baby in it, very gently. And as he did so, he remembered that it was not Christmas Eve any longer, but Christmas Day.

Then, carrying the box very carefully, he made his way slowly out of the church porch, and back across the waste ground, Jacko trotting at his heels. He couldn't hold the torch as well, so he put it at the bottom of the box, by the baby's feet.

Up the street, past the building site and the wharves and warehouses, empty and silent, towards the streets, and then the market, the shops, the Lane. His footsteps echoed.

The pubs and cafés had long since shut. The last trains had gone, and there were no cars on the main road.

Mr Hegarty walked on, stopping now and then to set the box down and rest his arms. Then Jacko stopped too, and waited patiently.

The baby had gone to sleep.

From across the last square, beside the bit of park, Mr Hegarty could see the lights shining out.

'Now then,' he said. But then, just for a minute, he didn't want to go on, didn't want to let the baby go. He felt a strange, half-sad, half-angry feeling, like a knot tightening inside him. Whoever could have left it in a box, in a cold porch, at Christmas? He looked down at it again. But then, because he knew there was only one right thing to do, he crossed the road and walked up the drive to the entrance.

'Stay,' he said. Jacko stayed.

Then, Mr Hegarty went through the glass doors into the lighted entrance of the King's Hospital.

In the hall, there was a huge Christmas tree, and paper chains and decorations strung from the ceiling and all around the walls. At the far end was a reception desk, with a porter behind it, and a nurse standing beside. Mr Hegarty went up to them and stood, holding the box in his arms.

'I've brought a baby,' he said.

In the next hour or so, a lot of things happened. The baby was taken away and Mr Hegarty asked to sit down, and answer a great many questions, from a nurse, and a doctor and finally, from two policemen. They brought him a cup of tea, and then another, with a pink bun, and asked him to sign some papers, and the whole time, Jacko sat without moving or barking, on the step beyond the glass doors. But in the end, the nurse came back again and said, 'You can go now, Mr Hegarty. You must be tired out.'

'Right,' said the policemen. 'We'll drop you off. Trafalgar Street, isn't it?'

Mr Hegarty stood up. He was tired, tired enough to drop, and muddled and in a way, sad.

'No, thank you very much,' he said. 'If it's all the same to you, I'll walk.' And he went slowly across the blue carpet to the glass doors, where Jacko was waiting.

'Come on, then,' said Mr Hegarty. Jacko came.

He did sleep, just a bit, but it was a strange, restless sleep, full of odd dreams and noises.

When he woke properly, it was just coming light. Grey. Damp looking. 'Happy Christmas, Jacko.' Mr Hegarty said. Jacko hardly stirred.

He was going to make a pot of tea, and then open his present from Jo. But, as he washed, he knew that he wouldn't, not yet. Knew that he would have to go there first, straight away, because the baby had been on his mind all night, and he couldn't settle until he'd made sure about it.

He let Cat in, whistled to Jacko, and crossed the streets all over again, in the same direction as before. And as he walked, he wondered. Whose baby? When? How? Why? What would happen to it now? He hadn't even found out what it was, girl or boy, hadn't liked to ask.

The hospital looked different in the early morning light, larger, greyer, somehow less friendly.

But he left Jacko on the step again, and went in, down the blue carpet.

After he had explained, they left him, sitting on a chair in a corridor. The hospital was still quiet, but not like the night before, he could hear doors banging and the lift going up and down.

Perhaps they would bring him a cup of tea again. He always had one as soon as he got up. He was missing it now.

But it didn't really matter. He'd had to come.

'Mr Hegarty?'

Mr Hegarty stood up.

'Would you like to come with me?'

Through doors. Down a corridor.

'I'm sure you'd like to see him wouldn't you?'

Him. A boy then. Yes, that was as it should be.

'He's fine, thanks to you. But if you hadn't found him...'

They went down more corridors. Around corners. Through doors. Stopped.

'You'll see that we've done something special,' she said.

'We always wait for the first baby born in the hospital on Christmas Day, but there hadn't been one yet. And besides, we thought that your baby was the most important one here today. Come in and see.'

There were babies in small cots. Through a glass window, he could see beds.

'Look, Mr Hegarty.'

At the end of the room, on a small, raised platform, stood a crib, draped and decorated, under a canopy. Hanging above the canopy was a star. 'The Christmas crib,' she said. 'Only used once a year. Today.'

Mr Hegarty went a step closer. Looked down. And there he was, the baby from the cardboard box in the dark church porch, the baby he had found and carried here with Jacko. The Christmas baby.

For a while, Mr Hegarty didn't speak.

Then he said quietly, 'King of Kings. That's who he is. The King of Kings.'

And went, smiling, out of the nursery.

They did find him a cup of tea, and a breakfast too, and a plate of sausages for Jacko, and said they would be letting him know what happened to the baby, when there was any news.

'And you'll be welcome to come and see him you know,' the nurse said. 'Any day.'

'Thank you,' Mr Hegarty said. 'Thank you very much. I should like that.'

And then he went home, with Jacko trotting beside him, through the quiet early streets of Christmas morning.

The Christmas Boy

A story from Russia

JENNY ROBERTSON

Once a boy was born without sight or speech, nor was he able
to hear a single sound. He lived alone with his mother. Children,
coming home from school, from the woods or fields, would see
him sitting on the doorstep of his wooden house. 'There he is, deaf
as a post and dumb as a stone,' they'd say. And they threw fir
cones at him and pricked him with thorns and thistles. In summer
they poured water over him and pelted him with mud and dust.
In winter they threw snowballs.

The boy would try to protect himself with upraised arms, while
tears rolled down his face.

His mother, hearing the children laughing, straightened from
her work with a smile. 'The children are having a good time! It
must make my poor boy happy when they play with him.'

The boy's mother was always busy. She cooked and baked,
scrubbed and cleaned, carried water, chopped logs, while her son
was locked away in his dark, silent world. His bare feet told him:
'The hard thing, level, with cracks across it, that's where I can
walk.' For, of course, he didn't know the name of the floor of his
hut. Softness, sometimes wet and with a wonderful smell: that
was the grass where he would sit after rain. He liked that sweet-
smelling softness just as he liked the feel of the soft warm cover
he lay beneath in winter nights.

Yes, he liked soft things, but he didn't much like the rough
woollen threads which his mother wound around his outstretched
hands when he had to sit still for a long time without moving his
fingers – he didn't know why.

Mother, he thought, is those wet drops which fall on my head
when she bends over me, a bit like the ones I feel when I'm sitting
outside and wetness comes. Mother – is caresses, kisses; and
sometimes something hard which hurts – I don't know why –
followed by those wet drops, more kisses, hugs. Mother – is nice

209

things in my mouth, a good full feeling inside.

What else? Sometimes it's warm, and I sit outside; or else it's the opposite: cold, and I stay indoors beside the fire. Sometimes, when I'm lying under my cover I stop feeling anything; then that passes; I get up and everything goes on as usual.

Yes, just as usual; but animals, birds and insects were kinder to the boy than the village children. Finches and chaffinches settled on his hands and shoulders: he felt the fluttering of their wings, felt their beaks pecking him with sharp kisses. Butterflies were his playthings, they brushed against his ears, his fingers. Cats snoozed in his lap: he loved the soft warmth of their bodies, loved the rhythm of their purring. Mice tickled his toes; squirrels curled round his knees; dogs licked him with friendly tongues; pet lambs snuggled against him; he picked them up and they laid their curly heads against his chest.

So the boy lived out his quiet, dark, silent days, until something happened which he remembered for the rest of his life.

It was winter. The frost was so severe that the boy stayed inside, and even so he could never feel warm. Suddenly the door opened – icy air blew around him and he shivered. The village children ran in, seized him and dragged him outside. 'Where are they taking me?' he wondered. Barefoot, wearing only the thinnest clothes, shaking with cold and fear, the boy was caught up in a stampede of children. Sometimes he fell. Feet trampled him, hands raised him and the children raced on, dragging the boy with them, further from home than he had ever been in his life.

But finally they came to a halt. The boy stretched out his hands. His fingertips touched something solid – it was a door and the children opened it. They pushed him inside. The air felt like summer all about him and he smelt the familiar, pleasant scent of hay. Doves flew to the boy. He felt the flutter of their wings – only these were not doves, but angels, and as soon as they touched his ears, everything which had been sealed and silent spoke. The boy could hear. He heard the children whispering around him. His ears caught the sound of the wind outside. From beneath his feet came the scratching, rustling sound of mice in search of food. Cows lowed, and the boy listened, filled with wonder. There came to his ears the cry of a child, so little and defenceless it made the boy think of the lambs which snuggled to him each spring. Suddenly the sound of singing, golden, shining, filled the boy with enchantment. The music rose and fell like the waves of a mighty ocean, now louder, now softer; and the majestic, triumphant sound filled the boy with delight. At length the golden voices fell silent; but now he heard a single voice, tender as the music of a silver flute: a mother sang a lullaby to her child, gentle, low... softly, more softly... until the boy was muffled in silence once again.

But now the dove-angels touched him a second time and the dark curtains of his sight opened. The boy saw that he stood inside a shadowy stable lit by a single trembling lantern flame. He saw the faces of the village children: full of wondering innocence. He saw the shapes of lowing cattle and marvelled that he now knew the sound those deep throats made. And, right beside a place for feeding cattle, which had now been made into a cot where a baby might lie, was a little grey mouse sitting so still it hardly twitched its long, thin whiskers, and certainly didn't seem at all frightened of rough hillmen, shepherds, perhaps, who had gathered about the manger too. Beside the men from the hills the boy saw the figure of a man who, with his young wife looked with wonder at the tiny, newborn baby she held in her arms. The boy looked too, for he had heard the lullaby the mother sang. Her radiant eyes sought the newly-opened eyes of the village boy. He could no longer hear but it seemed that she was calling him: 'Come, don't be afraid, come closer...'

The boy obeyed; and the village children stared in surprise for he no longer needed to stumble with searching fingers. It was as though a thousand stars filled the stable and lit his way. And the mother, smiling, held out her child. Hardly daring to breathe, the boy took the newborn baby into his arms... All of a sudden the baby opened his eyes and the boy who had been blind gazed at a light purer than the first rays of dawn, purer than newly-fallen snow – the boy couldn't imagine or name such light. It was as if the brightness of the singing he had heard, the brightness of a thousand stars flooded his whole being... but even as he smiled, the light faded and the world plunged into darkness once more.

The mother bent towards the boy to take her child. Her cloak brushed his hair. She kissed his forehead, his lips. The boy, trembling, uttered a cry which echoed through the stable; and at the sound of his voice the shepherds lifted him in their strong arms, wrapped him in their thick coats and carried him home. 'Don't be afraid,' they told his mother. 'Your son has heard the singing of angels; he has taken a newborn child, frail as a winter lamb, into his arms. Believe us, the sound he uttered then was a single golden trumpet call: we heard his voice ourselves.'

'Do you think I believe that kind of fairy story?' the boy's mother laughed. 'Look at him, he can't understand a single thing.'

But when the children came running home they told her everything the shepherds had said was true; and often, afterwards, the boy would press both hands against his chest; his face would light up with a smile, and the children would say, 'He's listening to the angels again, and he's looking at the baby he held in his arms, the baby who was born in a stable where cattle low and mice rustle.'

They didn't tease or torment the boy any more; instead they brought him gifts: berries and mushrooms from the forest, sweet-smelling meadow herbs, cakes they'd made at school. They knitted him socks of soft lambswool and wove slippers from strips of bark from slim silver birches. They crowned him with diadems of fresh spring flowers; in autumn they adorned his head with wreaths of rustling leaves, and in winter they mounted him on their sledges and gave him rides over crisp, smooth snow. The boy laughed with them and loved them, but most of all he loved the lambs which nuzzled to him, reminding him of the baby he had held in his arms, whose eyes had shown him the light of a thousand stars.

The Snow Kitten

NINA WARNER HOOKE

*No one wanted the hungry and abandoned snow kitten. But
the children cared, and they tried to work a miracle
in time for Christmas.*

The kitten had eaten no more than a mouthful before it was set
upon by the gulls, who had now been joined by a company of
rooks and jackdaws. Buffeted on all sides, twice knocked off its
feet and terrified by the savage pecks aimed at its eyes, the kitten
ran off to its old retreat under the wall. Here it crouched and
watched while the squawking quarrelling gang emptied the basin
and flew off.

After wandering aimlessly about for the rest of the day it went
back to the shed. Having been homeless for a fortnight it was
content to have found at least a dry sleeping place.

The Reece children had seen the rooks and gulls attacking the
kitten and would have run out to chase them away, but by the
time they had changed their shoes and put on their coats and
mufflers the birds had gone, leaving nothing but an empty
basin.

'Are there any more scraps?' Jinny asked her mother.

'No, there aren't. Not till tomorrow.'

'The birds took it all, Mum.'

'They're hungry too.'

'The kitten's awful thin, Mum.'

'So are other creatures. 'Tis hungry weather.'

'Any bread, is there?'

'Not to spare, or you'll get none for your supper.'

'I don't mind.'

'Speak for yourself, child. The others will.'

'Mum, couldn't we, *please* – '

'No.'

Mrs Trim's two cats, from their vantage point between the

flowerpots in the parlor window, had also watched the skirmish in front of the cottages. When it was over they yawned, jumped down, settled into an armchair on a pile of knitting and washed each other's ears.

The kitten, curled on the old potato sack, dozed away the afternoon. With twilight and darkness came something that compensated for hunger, loneliness and cold, a jewel that shone for it alone. Hour after hour, with its head resting peacefully on its paws, it gazed at Miss Coker's golden window.

It tried twice more to snatch a meal against vicious competition, and then gave up and did not leave the shed at all.

Miss Coker made it a rigid rule not to allow her mind to dwell on the past. It was a closed book, never to be opened. But having been reminded so sharply of her father that morning she could not stop thinking about him. And from him her thoughts wandered to other members of her family – to her mother, her dear mother, and her sister Lorna who was a schoolteacher and had just become engaged to a merchant navy officer. She even found herself thinking about the cat which had saved her life by running away before the fire. How extraordinary that it should have run off like that! Did it know what was going to happen? Had it had some mysterious warning? Cats were strange creatures. She remembered the day her sister brought it home from the local pet shop, just six weeks old and black as coal. It was a time when they were going through some trouble, she couldn't recall exactly what.

'His name is Sooty,' Lorna said. 'He's going to bring us luck.'

And so he did, it seemed, for many years until – until the morning when her mother said 'Have you seen Sooty? He didn't come in last night. I'm a bit worried. He's never stayed out so long before.'

The day wore on and still he didn't appear. They all went into the garden and called and called. After tea Miss Coker went out to search the streets. Lorna said, 'I'd come with you, but I've got some papers to correct.'

She walked a long way, asking in the local shops if anyone had found a black cat or reported an injured one. And then there was the glow in the sky, and the fire engines, and everyone running – a gas explosion they said, in the basement. She jerked her mind back to the present, sat for a moment with her eyes closed and her hands tightly clenched; then rose and put on the kettle for her tea.

Jinny was a persistent child...
She said to Joey, 'There's only us, so we got to do it.'
'Do what then?'
'Feed the kitten in Miss Coker's shed.'
'How we going to get the food? Our Mum won't give us nothin'.'
'I'll show you.'
Jinny's plan was simple. Unfortunately it miscarried. At the first attempt, the pair of them had been caught redhanded filching scraps from the Trims' chicken pail, and their reward was an afternoon of chopping sticks in Mr Trim's woodshed.

'Ain't we done enough yet?' Joey wailed. 'I'm cold. I want my tea.'
'You heard what he said. We got to fill the box.'
It was a huge box and by four o'clock when the light was failing they were still at it. Mrs Trim brought them mugs of hot milk.
'If it was me I'd let you off,' she said. 'But Dad gits so mad. And it's not as if you done the little cat any good. Them pesky gulls take all you put out.'
'We wasn't going to put it out,' Jinny said. 'We was going to take it to Miss Coker's shed where the kitten sleeps.'
'God bless me, don't you go trespassin' there. You'll get into worse trouble.'
After Mrs Trim had gone back indoors Jinny burst out crossly, 'It's *her* fault. That old Miss Coker. Why don't she feed the kitten? Why don't she take it in? Why does she have to be so mean?'

It was Christmas Eve. Shortly before supper time Miss Coker suddenly rose from her chair, took the torch and went out to the shed.
As she approached the kitten stirred and raised its head. She stooped and passed her hand over its body.
She had to force herself to do it. This was the first time in more than thirty years that she had fondled a living creature. The touch of the soft fur caused something to happen inside her, some easing of the frozen heart. The kitten struggled to its feet, arching itself under her hand. The white parts of its coat were soiled with coal dust. She understood then that it was too weak to clean itself, let

alone go in search of food.

She straightened up, stood for a moment fighting the inclination, walked off and stopped halfway across the yard. She looked back and saw that the kitten had followed her.

It crouched in the snow a few steps away, the tail dragging, eyes unnaturally big in the starved face. It stole forward a trifle. A few more tottering steps took it to Miss Coker's feet where it halted, uncertain, hovering between hope and fear.

She bent and picked it up. It lay passive in her arms, its bony little head pressed against her chin. Light as a bird it seemed. The draggled fur under her hand was not only without warmth but without resilience, more like the coat of a dead creature than a live one. The feeble heartbeats of the small body emphasized the strength of her own. Standing there alone in the ice-bound hush of the winter night she was suddenly and deeply aware of being *alive*. She saw, as if for the first time, the brilliance of the stars, the glittering beauty of the snow.

At the same moment she heard a burst of childish voices close at hand.

'We three kings of Orien-tar!'

The unsteady altos soared and dipped. Behind them, faint but sweet, sounded a far-off chime of church bells.

Miss Coker waited a minute or two, listening intently, before re-entering her cottage. She closed the kitchen door and took from the peg behind it an old knitted shawl she used when she went to fill her coal scuttle or empty the rubbish bucket. Next she pulled from under the sink a square shallow box which had once held apples. Lining the box with the shawl she set it down near the stove and laid the kitten in it while she warmed some milk. She filled a saucer and held the kitten in her arms while it lapped.

In her meat safe was a slice of liver she had bought for her supper. She cut off a portion and chopped it small, listening all the time to the carol singers outside her gate, who had now switched to *The Holly and the Ivy*. She fed the raw liver to the kitten, a tiny piece at a time, with long waits in between. Before it was finished the singers stopped. They had forgotten the second verse.

Miss Coker stood up and took from the dresser the two bars of chocolate she had bought at the post office store. She picked up the kitten and carried it down the hall to her front door, opened the door and stood on the step, beckoning to the children. Very cold, they were just on the point of going home. They stared at her, round-eyed with amazement. She beckoned again and held out the chocolate bars. Slowly, unbelievingly, they came up the path to take them. Neither child said anything. Nor did she.

They raced off with their news, bursting in and nearly knocking over the table on which Bert was trying to mend his old radio, both talking at once.

'Mum, Mum, she's got the kitten! She had it in her arms when she give us the choc!'

'She got it, Mum – '

'It had milk on its whiskers!'

'Well, dang me,' said Bert. 'Wonders never cease. Thing is, will she keep it?'

'I'd say she will,' Amy Reece said. 'Hard to turn it out again once you take in a stray.'

'She's bound to keep it, Mum. She were *stroking* it!' Their mother beamed fondly on the rosy sparkling faces.

'Well, thank goodness for that. Now we can all have a happy Christmas. Off with you to bed.'

The Joy of Giving

JOHN GREENLEAF WHITTIER

Somehow, not only for Christmas
But all the long year through,
The joy that you give to others
Is the joy that comes back to you;
And the more you spend in blessing
The poor and lonely and sad,
The more of your heart's possessing
Returns to make you glad.

Christmas and Peter Moss

MARY SMALL

The waste ground close to the water's edge belonged to the Harbour Trust. Except for the gulls it was no good for anything.

Nearby, partly hidden by trees, stood a small stone cottage. Peter Moss lived there. Once he had been a ship's engineer and had travelled all over the world... a long time ago.

The cottage was old, much older than Peter Moss. His grandfather had built it back in the early days. Many times the council had tried to buy it to make way for new buildings, but it was not for sale. Peter Moss often wondered what would happen to it when he died. He had no family, only Bosun, his dog.

Every day, Peter Moss and Bosun walked down to the waste ground for exercise. Bosun was young and full of energy. He loved to chase the stones and sticks that his master threw for him. When the old man grew tired, he would stand leaning on his stick gazing across the water to the tall, skyscraper buildings of the city. Sometimes a container ship would pass on its way to the docks and there were always ferries coming and going. Peter Moss reckoned that he had the best view in the city. Yet, in spite of the bustle around him, he was lonely.

Every other day, except Sunday, Peter Moss made the long slow walk to the shops at the top of Clark Street to buy groceries. It always alarmed him to see the bulldozers busy so near to his home and more and more flats rising up to the sky, full of new people. No one took any notice of the old man; they were too busy, too worried about their own affairs.

'Christmas gets earlier and earlier every year!' Peter Moss muttered as he looked in the shop windows. It was the time of the year he dreaded the most, for he was a shy man and although he had money it could not buy him friends.

One Saturday morning he was surprised to see three youngsters with bikes walking around the waste ground talking together. They stayed there a long time and then went away.

On Sunday, more children came. They seemed very excited about something. They took spades and started to dig up the ground. Peter Moss stood at the window watching. He didn't like to interfere but they had no right to intrude. He waited a while, then opened the door and walked down with Bosun.

'What are you doing?' he asked. 'This land belongs to the Harbour Trust. You can't dig it up like that.'

'Why not?' said Glen, the biggest boy. 'It's not used for anything.'

'We need somewhere to ride our BMX bikes,' said Nikos.

'The street's no good,' said Werner, punching the ground with the heel of his boot.

'You'll get into big trouble if you do anything with it,' said Peter Moss.

'But we want to make a practice track with dips and jumps,' said Michelle. 'For that we need rough ground. This couldn't be better.'

All the youngsters stood and stared at him. Peter Moss didn't know what to do. 'You'll have to find somewhere else,' he said gruffly. Not wanting to argue, he called to Bosun and started to walk away. He could feel their strong resentment.

The youngsters muttered among themselves.

'There isn't anywhere!' shouted Glen angrily.

Peter Moss stopped. The children were right; for them there was nowhere. Youngsters nowadays didn't have the space he had when he was a boy.

'Watch it!' said Glen. 'Old Nosey-Parker's coming back!'

Spades in their hands, they stood and waited.

'I've just had a thought,' said Peter Moss. 'I'm on the Harbour Trust Board Committee. You leave the ground alone and I'll have a talk to them and maybe to the council too.'

'O.K. by us,' said Glen. 'When will you know?'

'That I can't say,' said Peter Moss. 'You'll have to be patient. Come back and see me later this week. I live in the cottage up there.'

The boys were at school when the people from the Harbour Trust came. They spent a long time looking at the land and a long time talking to Peter Moss. Then they went away. The old man felt sad. They hadn't made a decision one way or the other. He knew that if the children didn't get the land they'd blame it on him and go elsewhere.

'This sort of thing takes time,' he said when the children knocked on the door.

Just when he had almost given up hope, the telephone rang. As Peter Moss listened to the voice a big smile spread over his face.

'The kids will be delighted,' he said. 'Yes, I'll be only too pleased to keep an eye on things. I'm sure there'll be no trouble.'

So the children and their friends dug ditches and made jumps and a track for their BMXs.

As the days grew longer, the old man had company most evenings and all the weekends. It was impossible for him to be lonely. When they weren't riding the children would sit on the veranda and talk to him.

'When I was young they didn't make bikes like that,' said Peter Moss in amazement as Werner shot out from a ditch and twisted his bike in the air, and Nikos and Glen bounced over the whoopy-doos.

'They're very expensive,' said Elke. 'Gino and Francesco who live next to us are selling newspapers to buy them.'

'My brothers Jose and Mario are getting them for Christmas,' said Rosa, 'but you mustn't tell. It's a secret.'

'Nikos hopes to trade his for a better one,' said Sofie.

'No way can I get one,' said Richard. 'My dad's out of work.'

'Nor me,' said Paul. 'We haven't the money.'

From the conversations, Peter Moss was surprised that so many of the children living in the street came from different countries, places he knew quite well from his years at sea; Nikos and Sofie from Greece, Werner and Elke from Germany, Gino and Francesca from Italy, Jose, Mario and Rosa from South America, Michelle from France, Danny and Kate from England. He heard about Tuan and Khai who had come from Vietnam in an open boat.

'They live over the shop next to the Chinese restaurant,' said Kate. 'They seem very poor and can't speak much English.'

Peter Moss started to do a lot of thinking.

The Friday before Christmas, a white panel van pulled up at his house. When it had gone, Peter Moss went up the street to the hardware store. He bought a piece of chipboard, a small tin of paint and a brush. Then he went home and locked the door. He was busy all day.

Danny was the first to notice the sign hung on the veranda.

'Look!' he said, calling to the others. 'BMX BIKES FOR HIRE, NO CHARGE. Say! What has the old man done?'

Dropping their bikes, the children raced up to the cottage and banged on the door. Bosun barked as Peter Moss opened it.

'Happy Christmas!' he said. 'Come in and see!'

They crowded inside and there in a little back room stood four brand new bikes.

'For anyone who needs one,' said Peter Moss. 'I asked for the best in the shop.'

'They're sure good!' said Michelle. 'Look, snake-belly tyres, chrome-moly frames and all!'

Talking excitedly, the children jostled each other to hold the bikes.

'It's unreal!' said Glen. 'Gosh! Thanks a million. Wait'll we tell the others.'

Next evening, the children called a meeting at Werner's and Elke's house.

'What do you think he does at Christmas time?' they said. 'Probably nothing much.' Excitedly their talk continued.

On Christmas Eve, Peter Moss went to the shops early to buy food for himself and Bosun. Everyone smiled at him.

'Happy Christmas, Mr Moss!' they said. 'Happy Christmas!'

He had friends everywhere.

The waste ground lay silent and empty that evening. Peter Moss had just sat down to tea when Bosun growled softly. There was a noise of feet shuffling on the veranda, then suddenly voices started singing. Peter Moss went to the door and opened it. There stood Nikos and Sofie and all their Greek friends. Peter Moss had never heard a song so beautiful.

'Happy Christmas, Mr Moss!' sang out Rosa, and the carol singers moved aside so that her brothers Jose and Mario could carry a Christmas tree into the house. They placed it in a corner of the kitchen and the visitors crowded round, covering it with goodies and decorations.

'Our dad reckoned you'd need some good cheer,' said Danny and Kate, putting a bottle of whisky under the tree.

'And I bought a new collar for Bosun,' said Richard.

'And I've brought him biscuits,' said Paul.

'You must eat this tonight,' said Elke, placing a cake plaited and covered with icing on the table. 'We call it a *stollen*. Gino and Francesco have something for you too,' and the Italian boys came forward with a dish full of delicious-looking toffee.

'It's *torrone*,' said Gino. 'Mum made it from almonds and sugar and honey. She sends you good wishes.'

Mike went to the door and pushed Tuan and Khai towards the old man. They held out a lighted lantern made from paper and smiled shyly.

'It's from their Moon Festival,' said Werner. 'They want you to have it.'

'You're invited to dinner at our place tomorrow,' said Glen and Donna. 'Roast turkey, plum pudding, the lot. Did you have anything planned? We'll fetch you at midday.'

'We must hurry,' said Rosa, 'for we have our dinner tonight after church.'

'We have ours too!' said Francesco.

'And so do we!' said Elke and Sofie.

Peter Moss sat down in his chair at the table. He looked at the children and the bright things around him. There were tears in his eyes.

'Thank you,' he said very softly. 'It's the most wonderful Christmas I've ever had.'

Acknowledgments

Thanks go to all those who have given permission to include material in this book, as indicated in the list below. Every effort has been made to trace and contact copyright owners. We apologize for any inadvertent omissions or errors.

'Getting Ready for Christmas', copyright © Rachel Anderson 1991. Reprinted from *Happy Christmas, Little Angel* by Rachel Anderson (1991) by permission of Oxford University Press. 'The Spider's Web' by William Barclay from *The Daily Study Bible (Matthew)*. Reprinted by permission of The Saint Andrew Press. 'Papa Panov's Special Christmas' by Mary Batchelor, copyright © 1984, from *The Lion Christmas Book*. 'The Christmas in Mama's Kitchen' by Jean Bell Mosley, reprinted with permission from *Guideposts Family Christmas Book*, 1980. Copyright © 1980 by Guideposts, Carmel, NY 10512, USA. 'Nativity Play Plan' (3311, pp. 102-103) from *When I Dance: Poems by James Berry* (Hamish Hamilton Children's Books, 1988) copyright © 1988 by James Berry. 'Nativity Play' by Clare Bevan, copyright © 1996. 'Good King Wenceslas', 'St Boniface and the Christmas Tree' and 'The First Christingle' by Marilyn Bruce, copyright © 1996. 'A Greeting' and 'The Naughty Donkey', copyright © 1965 by Agatha Christie Mallowan. 'Trouble at the Inn' by Dina Donohue, reprinted with permission from *Guideposts Magazine*. Copyright © 1966 by Guideposts, Carmel, NY 10512, USA. 'The First Christmas' by Timothy Dudley-Smith from *The Lion Book of Stories of Jesus*, published by Lion Publishing plc. *Caspar and the Star* by Francesca Bosca. Copyright © 1991 Edizioni San Paolo S.r.l. *The Singing Shepherd* by Angela Elwell Hunt, copyright © 1992. Used by permission of Lion Publishing U.S. 'A Time Like This' copyright © 1989 by Madeleine L'Engle. Reprinted by permission. 'What the Donkey Saw' copyright © U. A. Fanthorpe from *Poems for Christmas* (Peterloo Poets, 1980), reproduced with permission. 'The Journey of the Three' by Elizabeth Gibson, copyright © 1996. 'The Surprise' and 'A Night the Stars Danced for Joy' from *Angels, Angels All Around* by Bob Hartman, copyright © 1993. Used by permission of Lion Publishing U.S. 'King of Kings' from *The Christmas Collection*. Text copyright © 1993 Susan Hill. Reprinted by permission of the publisher Walker Books Ltd, London. 'Carol of the Brown King' by Langston Hughes from *Selected Poems*, Vintage; from *Collected Poems* by Langston Hughes, copyright © 1994 by the Estate of Langston Hughes. Reprinted by permission of Alfred A. Knopf, Inc. (US). 'Not To Be Opened Before December XXV' by Nan Hunt, first published 1988 in *We Got Wheels, Man* by William Collins Pty Ltd, Sydney, in association with Anne Ingram Books. 'Christmas at the Little House in the Big Woods' from *The Little House in the Big Woods*, Methuen Children's Books, copyright © 1932 by Laura Ingalls Wilder. Copyright renewed 1959 by Roger L. MacBride. 'I was there!' (originally entitled 'Seth') by David Kossoff from *Book of Witnesses*, published by Harper-Collins Publishers Ltd. 'Christmas Comes to Narnia' from *The Lion, the Witch and the Wardrobe* by C. S. Lewis, published by HarperCollins Publishers Ltd. 'How We Lived Then' by Norman Longmate, published by Hutchinson, 1971. Text of *The Christmas Donkey* by Gillian McClure, copyright © 1993, published by Scholastic Ltd. 'If' by Janey Mitson, copyright © The National Exhibition of Children's Art. 'Kippy Koala's Christmas Present' by Win Morgan, copyright © 1987. Reprinted by permission of Albatross Books Pty Ltd. 'King for a Day' by Ruth Newman, copyright © 1996. 'A Bright Star Shone' by Janis Priestley from *Whispering in God's Ear*, published by Lion Publishing plc. 'Little Brown Jesus' by Joan O'Donovan from *Goodnight Stories*, published by Pan Piccolo, 1982. 'The Christmas Boy' by Jenny Robertson, copyright © 1996. Extracts from Revised English Bible © Oxford University and Cambridge University Presses 1989. Extract from *The Worst Kids in the World/The Best Christmas Pageant Ever* by Barbara Robinson reproduced by permission of the publishers Faber and Faber Ltd (UK) and of A.P. Watt Ltd (US). 'Christmas Joy' by Helen Robinson, copyright © The National Exhibition of Children's Art. Extract from *Chris and the Dragon* by Fay Sampson, copyright © 1985. Reprinted by permission of Victor Gollancz Ltd. *Baboushka* by Arthur Scholey, copyright © 1982, published by Lion Publishing plc. Extract from *A Vicarage Christmas* by Noel Streatfeild, copyright © Noel Streatfeild. Reproduced by permission of A.M. Heath & Company Ltd. 'The Three Wise Men' from *John Barleycorn* and 'A Farmhouse Christmas' from *The Country Child* by Alison Uttley, published by Faber and Faber Ltd. 'A Mouse and a Song' by Jean Watson, copyright © 1996. 'Christmas Tree' Words & Music: William James/John Wheeler (W/C 100%) © Copyright 1961 Chappell & Co (Australia) Pty Ltd (AM). For Australia & New Zealand: Warner/Chappell Music Pty Ltd (A.C.N. 000 876 068) 1 Cassins Avenue, North Sydney NSW 2060. International Copyright Secured. All Rights Reserved. Unauthorized Reproduction Is Illegal.